STUMBLING BACKASSWARDS INTO THE LIGHT

STUMBLING BACKASSWARDS INTO THE LIGHT

JAY NORRY

Stumbling Backasswards Into The Light
Copyright © 2001 by Jay Norry

Cover Concept: Jay Norry
Cover Design by: Dawn Norry
Author Photo by: Portia Shao

Publishers note:
This book is a work of fiction. Names, characters, places and incidents are either the product of the author's imagination or are used fictitiously, and any resemblance to actual persons living or dead, events, or locales is entirely coincidental.

All rights reserved. No part of this book may be reproduced in any form by any electronic or mechanical means including photocopying, recording, or information storage and retrieval without permission in writing from the author.

Paperback edition
ISBN-13: 978-0-9907280-1-6
ISBN-10: 0-9907280-1-3

www.SuddenInsightPublishing.com
Indie Publishing for the Indie Author

Acknowledgements

So many people have been a part of this book becoming something more than just a collection of ideas knocking around in my head, I would like to take this opportunity to express my gratitude…

Thank you, Dad, for being both a perfect father and a perfect friend to me.

Thank you, Shawna, for loving your odd brother just as I am, and for relating so genuinely to me.

Thank you, Richard Bach. Though I have never met you, this book would not have been written if not for you having the courage to share so much of yourself, with me and this world.

Thank you, Joel, for the soul-shaking messages and heartfelt encouragement.

Thank you, Dawn, for bringing this book into the 21st century.

Special thanks to my Mom, not just for being exactly the mother I need, but for believing in my dream and being a part of making it a reality.

Can you thank the Light? Yeah, sure, you can thank the Light…thanks, God. You rock.

For Dee . . .

CHAPTER ONE

Ghosts. They drifted in and out of the periphery of my vision, taunting me with their shapeless forms and formless shapes. Paralysed with fear, all I could do was cringe internally, and cringe I did.

I felt them more than I saw them, and they were my demons, and in their feeling was death…cold, cruel, and uncaring. Death was here to claim my wasted life, to reclaim the chance I hadn't earned. He was eager to encircle bony, lifeless hands around my throat.

My apprehension grew as the ghosts began whispering. Hissing, hateful voices ticked off my failures, one by one, and they brought with them scenes from my life. Mercilessly, incessantly, the voices drilled painfully into my head.

I clapped my hands over my ears, but the voices found their way into my head, became more insistent still…

Eyes closed tightly, the scenes grew only more vivid, more colorful, more real…

Tears streamed unchecked down my cheeks, and my body began to shake convulsively. The voices grew impossibly loud, and every cold accusation was a dagger in my skull.

I tried to speak, to scream, to beg them to stop, but all that escaped my lips was a wretched sob, then another.

There was only one avenue of escape. I sensed him behind me, watching my torment with calm and sickening glee.

I whirled to face him, took an instinctive step backward as I beheld the face of Death. Hollow eye sockets bored their gaze into my soul from under a menacing black hood. His skull was lifeless, and more: I felt a loathing of life, a hate so powerful it seemed to be consuming me, bit by bit, the longer I held his irresistibly terrible gaze.

I forced myself to take a step toward him, and felt a wall of fear that hit me like a physical blow. I stood trembling for a moment, steeled myself, then took another step.

My stomach twisted in a knot of revulsion; but even as I doubled over in pain, I forced myself forward another agonizing step. I fell at his feet finally, my breath coming in short, quick gasps.

Eyes begging for mercy, I looked up at him. Not a hint of compassion came from the skull's eyeless sockets. He mocked my pain, even seemed to *feed* off it.

I tried to drag my body closer, only to collapse again.

Hopelessly, pleadingly, I reached out to him, begging with my eyes shamelessly: *end it, just end it, please!*

Finally, he responded.

Slowly, purposefully, mockingly, he stepped forward, reaching for my outstretched hand. As he grasped my hand with a cold, viselike grip…

* * *

I awoke, a scream caught in my throat. Sitting up with a start, I hit my head on hard glass, collapsed onto the cold blankets I had cast off in my sleep. Shivering, wiping tears from my face, I breathed deep, tried to calm myself. As my mind came fully awake, I became aware once again of my predicament. Hopelessness came crashing in on me. I frowned fiercely against more tears.

Shaking violently from the cold, I wrapped the blankets tightly about my body. I curled up in the fetal position, partly because it was so cold and partly because I didn't have room to stretch out: I was sleeping in the back of my car.

Thankful for my accidental foresight in buying a hatchback, I had pushed the back seat forward. That gave me enough room for nearly everything I owned and a makeshift bed.

I snorted in self-disgust, appalled that I should be thankful that my car was accommodating enough to also be my home. A month ago I'd have never considered it a possibility; now it was my reality.

Pulling the blankets closer, I tried to push my own thoughts from my mind. It didn't matter why I was here, it didn't matter what I did wrong or what I should have done right. It didn't matter that tomorrow scared me more than that terrifying nightmare.

Sleep was my only escape, my only reprieve; and now even my dreams were being tainted by my hopelessness. As it stole over me again, I heard the whispering, hissing voices that assured me I would find no peace tonight.

CHAPTER TWO

I awoke the next morning to car doors slamming and accompanying voices. Moaning, I tried to roll over, only to painfully ram my knee into a crate of clothes. I tried to rub my knee and bury my face in the pillow at the same time.

More sleep was what I wanted, what I really needed, but I knew I couldn't get that here, in the parking lot of a grocery store. In the back of my car.

Head pounding, body aching, I wiped a circle in the condensation that clung to the inside of the window. I raised bleary and bloodshot eyes, reluctantly, to face the day.

It was raining.

At least I still had a few cigarettes. Three, to be exact. I lit one, then spent the next several minutes rifling through the trash on the floor of my car looking for change.

Seventy-eight cents. Seventy-eight goddamned cents to my goddamned name. I cursed under my breath.

Clenching my jaw, I started my car, waited for the gas gauge to rise. It stopped before it started, resting firmly on "E."

That did it.

Sobbing, incoherent, I dutifully used every curse I knew in a high, shrieking voice that was not my own. I was frightening *myself*, but I still didn't seem to want to stop.

Then I caught something out of the corner of my eye, people. Curious, a small group had stopped in their tracks to watch the young man who had mistakenly thought he was alone with his insanity.

"Fuck you!" I screamed in that strange, scary voice. "Fuck you all!"

I slammed my car into gear and squealed the tires all the way to the street.

The girl behind the counter at the gas station was chewing gum and twisting a lock of hair absently around her index finger. She looked down at my little collection of coins on the counter and smirked. She started to open her mouth to make some comment; but at that moment, she looked up and into my eyes.

Her face went lax, the comment died on her lips.

Smart girl, I thought.

"Seventy-eight cents on pump number four," I hissed.

She nodded, still not speaking, counted the change.

Then I was headed for the freeway, as I heard my stomach start to wake up. I hadn't eaten for some three days now. All I could do was to ignore it as best I could, as I had to ignore my mind protesting with its practical concerns as I pulled onto the freeway.

My family had moved to Montana when I was young. We lived among the majestic beauty of the mountains and trees in the northwest region of the state until I became a legal adult and moved immediately west to Seattle.

From the day we moved there, I hated Montana. I cursed it whenever I got the chance, because I had never wanted to live there. But Montana had gotten to me in one way, one way I'll never forget. Among the expected hard winters and short summers and rednecks, there was one saving grace I had never expected: the woods.

In the woods I felt calm, hiking for hours, climbing trees and rock faces nearly every day, sometimes all day. I had always felt a kind of kinship there among the patient nobility of the trees and the quietly restless murmuring of the creeks. It sounded corny to me even as I thought about it, but the closest I had ever come to a feeling of peace was alone in the silence of a forest.

So I headed east on I-90, away from the city I had so eagerly set out for what seemed like lifetimes ago.

I had to keep continually pushing so many voices to the back of my mind. Not enough gas to get back to town, no money to even buy food, just go back to…

But there was nothing *to* go back to. Something had snapped inside of me, and I knew I couldn't be around any of that, any of those people anymore.

I just didn't care. I didn't care about any of it anymore.

It seemed strange to have to keep reminding myself of that, again and again.

So I screamed then, screamed at the top of my lungs like the madman I felt like. I screamed until I coughed, cleared my throat, started screaming again. It drowned out the voices in my head a little bit. And to tell the truth, it felt kind of good, and I thought, *I wonder if one could consciously and purposefully drive oneself out of one's own mind, screaming oneself into complete insanity…*

* * *

The car's engine sputtered once, twice, then came back full power as I coasted down the exit ramp. I shook my head, amazed that I had reached my destination at all.

I parked, turned the key off and closed my eyes gratefully, in exhaustion.

After a few moments, I opened my eyes and looked around. I remembered then why this place had come to mind. Friends had brought me here a couple of times, and it had struck me as too natural of a setting to be called a park. Far from untouched by man, you could almost fool yourself into thinking it was wilderness if you broke trail.

I sat behind the wheel, engine ticking, and smoked my second-to-last cigarette. I sat there until my mind starting asking just what I thought I was doing. Angrily, defiantly, I stubbed out my cigarette and got out of the car, locking it behind me.

Spots swam in front of my eyes for a moment, and I had to put my hand on the hood to steady myself. My makeshift bed in the back of the car caught my eye and I stared at it longingly, then shook my head. I'd come back later to get more rest. Right now, while it was daylight and not really raining, I had to get something in my stomach.

Despite the years growing up in Montana, the only thing I knew I could eat for sure were wild blackberries. Everything else was at least *somewhat* questionable, and my stomach was not up for experimentation. It was, however, making constant gurgling and groaning noises, and starting to spasm from time to time. Of course, that wasn't just the hunger, either. More than a little anxiety laced my every thought.

Up the trail, there was a bridge over a small but strong creek. I sidestepped the bridge and walked to the water's edge. Kneeling down, bending over to get a drink, I flinched.

My own reflection, and I couldn't bear to look at it. I forced myself to, though, to examine the dark half-circles under my eyes. And my eyes, usually a bright blue, were now sunken and milky, dull and lifeless. My complexion could kindly be described as sallow, and my long blond hair hung limp, stringy and unwashed.

I made myself look, for a long time, thinking how much I looked like a corpse already. I hated myself for being here, for letting things get so far out of hand. It had been a long time since I had looked myself in the eye; and as I did, a tear escaped from one eye and slid slowly down my cheek.

Standing abruptly, I wiped the tear away with the back of my sleeve. I swayed a bit as another wave of dizziness came over me.

Shaking my head to clear it, I started up the steep incline of the nearest trailhead.

I regretted it immediately. Tired, sore, burned

out, my legs moaned in agony. Punishing myself, I pushed onward. I broke a sweat too quickly, but was too dehydrated to maintain it. My eyesight got blurry, then cleared, faded, came back. As it started to fade again, I tripped on a rock and fell to one knee.

I stayed that way a full minute, head down, forearm on one knee, other knee on the ground. Standing slowly this time, my vision was clear, and I remembered:

Blackberry bushes hedged the trail on both sides. Looking back the way I'd come, I saw that I had passed dozens of them in my self-absorbed frenzy to find them.

Like an animal, I pounced, picking with both hands and ravenously shoving them into my mouth one after another. Rivulets of juice ran down my chin, dripping to stain my shirt. I paid no mind to anything but the taste of *food*, finally. After three days, anything can taste like heaven…

* * *

Twenty minutes later, I was on my hands and knees, vomiting painfully until I had parted company with every last berry. I rolled over onto my back afterward, eyes closed, trying to think of something I could eat. After a few minutes, I just stopped being hungry. Apparently my stomach had given up on me. Fine by me.

Lifting myself slowly from the ground, I dragged my tired body back down the trail. I felt old, so old I could *feel* myself dying. It took my last reserves of strength to half-walk, half-stumble back to the edge of the creek.

Careful not to look at my reflection, I knelt and leaned over the water. I submerged my face completely. A few quick gulps of the ice-cold water, then I felt bubbles tickle my cheeks as the air escaped my lungs.

This is the way to die, they say, I thought casually. *Just breathe in real deep; then you feel all calm and peaceful for a minute, then everything goes black.*

I lifted my face slowly from the water, wondering where on Earth that thought had come from.

"That's just not like me," I said aloud, my voice a little shaky, "To contemplate suicide when I still have a cigarette left."

My voice sounded strange there by the water, somehow unnatural.

Even more unnatural was the sound of my lighter, the soft click as sparks were cast into the path of the butane. I chuckled softly at my own off-color humor as the tobacco caught fire, inhaled deeply. Exhaling ringlets of smoke, I wondered if that had been my subconscious intention, coming all this way.

I shrugged. *If I'm going to die, better on grass than concrete,* I mused silently. *At least here my body would go to good use, dragged away and eaten by bear or coyote. If I died among people, the idiots would either incinerate it or bury it in a box, no use to anyone.*

An image formed in my head of a headstone over an empty grave, epitaph brazenly stating: "Here lies Jay. Unremarkable in every attempted endeavor save being a tasty appetizer."

Sprawled on my back, I smoked and gazed at the clouds that drifted lazily by.

At least my stomach wasn't demanding

anything. Apparently we were no longer on speaking terms, it being so unimpressed with my pathetic attempt to fulfill its simple request.

For a moment, there on my back in the grass, I thought I felt something akin to contentment. As the unfinished cigarette slipped from my fingers, it manifested as sheer exhaustion, and my eyes closed.

CHAPTER THREE

I awoke slowly in what appeared to be a cave. Sparing light from a crackling open fire cast long shadows on rock walls. It was hard to see much beyond the stack of wood near the fire, but what I could see I liked.

Candles were everywhere, dark and dormant, affixed with their own wax to natural shelves of stone. Tapestries with indistinguishable patterns hung at regular intervals.

And books. Shelves of books, stacks of them, all over the place.

The smell of wood heat filled my nostrils warmly, but no smoke. Curious, I cocked my head to better see the fire, squinted. As I watched, a tendril of smoke drifted lazily but definitely to a series of fissures in the ceiling and disappeared naturally.

I grinned. Well, at least my dreams were getting good again.

Of course, soon I would wake by the river's edge only to spend my last moments warding off impatient scavengers. *That* I was not looking forward to.

Right now, though, I could contentedly survey the cozy little scene my subconscious mind had created.

Noticing for the first time the bed I was lying in, I sunk more deeply into it. Blankets and pillows and furs were stacked one on top of the other in a big soft comfortable heap. Perfect.

And the more I stared into the darkness, the more I could make out. I saw a tree stump nearby, nature turned nightstand. A loaf of bread and a small basket of fruit adorned its smooth surface.

Blackberry memory still in mind, I reached past the fruit to seize the loaf of bread.

It was delicious. I tried to eat slowly, but half the loaf was gone before I knew it.

I nibbled at an apple then, cautiously, just to wash the bread down.

Lying back, I wondered what kind of dream this was, just lounging about while my body was starving thirty feet from my car.

Then I was waking up to my own loud snoring, turning on my side and drifting further off to sleep.

* * *

I woke again some time later, this time with a start. Not only was I still in the cave, I was not alone. A man was crouched with his back to me, stoking the fire.

Eyeing him cautiously, I tried to think of something to say. I opened my mouth once or twice, but couldn't seem to find my voice.

Meanwhile, he quietly and expertly stirred the

coals, then gently stacked the wood atop them. I thought then that he must be trying not to disturb me, and it surprised me when he spoke:

"When a man goes to great lengths to save another man's life, gratitude is generally the most socially acceptable response." His back still to me as he said it, his voice so calm and quiet, I couldn't tell if his sarcasm was good-natured or not. He leaned closer to the coals, blew gently until a flame winked into sudden existence.

"Uh, yeah, thanks," I stammered, still trying to get my bearings. I chided myself for sounding like an idiot.

He stood and turned to face me then, in one fluid motion, and I couldn't miss the smile dancing at the corners of his mouth. On the short side of tall, he was stockier than me at the shoulders and slimmer at the waist. Short black hair and a beard, flecked with gray, framed a face that struck me with an unusual openness.

His eyes seemed to sparkle as he watched me, watching him. I felt immediately at ease with him. He walked toward me with casual confidence and settled on a mat at the foot of my bed. Didn't say anything. Smiled, but didn't speak.

Remembering my manners, I leaned toward him, extending my hand. "Uh, it's, uh, nice to meet you, my name is—"

His laugh silenced me, a loud, mocking bark.

"Name?" He looked cold steel at me. "Name?! You have no name! I know why you came up here, you came here to die; to end the part of you, the *only* part of you, that is at all concerned with names. I may have stopped that from happening, but that doesn't earn you your name back. Your name here is 'Nobody'."

No longer at ease, I sat up straight, rigid. "Well, I guess that makes *you* 'Somebody', is that right?" I sneered at him, defensive.

The hardness in his face melted, and he grinned. "I guess it does." I had meant the comment to be cutting, rudeness in answer to his bluntness. Somehow we both had agreed on it, like we had spoken some secret formula. From that moment forward, I never knew him or thought of him as anything else. Somehow that never seemed odd to me.

Still smiling, he stood and walked toward a passageway that wound swiftly around a sharp corner and out of sight. He turned to face me again.

"You need more rest, Nobody, and you need to feel safe to get it. You imagine that your safety relies on external sources, so let me assure you that I am indeed your friend and that I bear you nothing but good will."

That said, he turned again and walked swiftly away, down the passageway.

Stunned, I sat there for a full minute, staring after his departed steps. When it became obvious that he wasn't coming back any time soon, I swung my legs from under the covers to get up. There was another passage opposite the one he had gone through across the room. One or both of them had to be exits; and if this fellow got any weirder, I wanted to know which one. His intentions seemed to be good, sure, but I had seen plenty of good intentions go very bad in my life.

Sometimes the smartest thing one can know is where the nearest exit is.

Trying to stand, I realized that my exploratory mission would just have to wait. He was right, I did need more rest. My body still ached, and my mind was like bald tires on slick ice. This was all so weird…so much, so fast. I didn't have the presence of mind to grapple with it right now, and I was glad Somebody had left me alone.

Lying back again, I was suddenly glad for my decision to trust him. Comfortable, relaxed, I drifted off almost immediately.

* * *

During the next few days, everything blurred into everything else. Time passed strangely, even more so with nothing to gauge it by. No clocks hung on the walls, and the only light sources were internal, the candles and the fire. On rare occasion, a shaft of sunlight found its way inside, but not very often and never for long.

I drifted in and out of sleep, sometimes waking famished and sometimes sick and fevered. My mysterious rescuer brought me food and drink, always simple and always delicious.

I tried to explain myself a few times, why I was so thin, why I sometimes threw up perfectly good food. It was all my fault, and I didn't deserve his kindness.

But he always hushed me and told me to get more rest, or asked what I thought I *could* keep down.

"Plenty of time for that later, Nobody," he would say, smiling, leaving me alone to rest.

Then I awoke one night in the middle of the

day, yawned and stretched and smiled sleepily. I felt great.

I jumped.

He was sitting a few feet away, staring at me intently. I smiled, but he didn't react at all. I squirmed, inside, under his gaze, starting to feel quite uncomfortable, when he spoke:

"Nobody, tell me why you wanted to die." He said it simply, evenly, just a question he wanted answered.

Practicing then opening my mouth only to shut it again...I expected each time for something to come out, was relieved and disappointed each time nothing did.

Somebody sat and watched me silently, patiently, until it dawned on me that he was indeed going to wait until I spoke.

"I don't know if I really *wanted* to die," I said slowly. "I guess it was more like...more like I couldn't find a reason to live that seemed worth all the effort required."

He smiled then, a sad lonely little smile, and tears shone in his eyes. "And what led you to that conclusion?"

I tried to think back, couldn't. "I don't know," I answered. "I never really thought about it, I guess."

"Well, maybe you *shouldn't* think about it. Maybe you should talk about it." He leaned closer, spoke intently. "Try something for me, if you would. Put yourself there, just a few days back, to whatever led you my way. Then don't think, just talk."

I nodded, reluctantly. It was time to tell him.

"Well, the last year of my life has been the worst year of my life, by far. I sunk lower than I ever thought I would." I breathed deep, steeled myself.

"I have been doing heavy drugs for several months now, coke and crystal meth, whenever I could…which was most of the time."

I was quiet, awaiting his reaction. He just looked at me, unsurprised, nodded for me to go on.

"I hated myself for doing it, for being that, but I just couldn't seem to stop. I'd decide to quit, go to sleep, wake up feeling like death, and make that phone call. I hated myself when I was high, yeah, but I hated myself even more when I wasn't. It was driving me nuts."

It felt kind of good talking about it, but I began to feel that old doom feeling that seemed to always hang over my life as I went on:

"All my friends, nearly everyone I knew, were doing it. These were the people I worked with and hung out with. So I quit my job to change my life." I sighed.

"Worked, too. Changed my life, all right. I ran out of money, ran out of drugs, ran out of the friends I'd never really had…"

I trailed off, noticing the bitter tone that had crept into my voice, looked up to see if he had too.

Tears shone brightly in his eyes.

"I don't want your goddamned pity," I snapped. "I deserved everything I got. I deserved to wake up hungry and alone in the back of my car. I deserved the fate that I thought I was coming up here to face. The only thing I didn't deserve was you saving my life. My life was not worth the saving. Why do you even care?"

He looked at me then for a long time. The tears faded from his eyes, but the softness didn't. Finally, smiling, he leaned forward again.

"It's tough to know where to begin," he said. "Ever hear the phrase 'When the student is ready, the teacher will appear'?"

"Yeah, I have," I nodded. "All my life I loved to read, and lately I've read a couple of books about…"

I flushed, remembering people's reactions when they had seen what I'd been reading lately.

"…I read a couple of books that said something like that," I finished lamely.

He didn't notice my faltering, or pretended not to.

"Well, I guess that's kind of what's happening here," he said evenly.

"Look," I said, trying to keep the irritation out of my voice, "I appreciate you helping me out, for saving my life and all, but I'm right back where I started. I'm broke, I'm homeless, I've got very few options, if any. The drugs are out of my system, yeah, but that doesn't make me any less of a pathetic wretch. I don't need to learn your pet philosophies, I need to find a way to get back on my feet…or kill myself right."

He stood, put his hands resolutely on his hips. "Let me make you a little proposition: I'll promise you that everything will be taken care of, that you need worry about nothing while you are here with me. But you must promise me that you will give me a week to prove that I just may have something of immense value to impart."

I started to respond that it wasn't that simple, it couldn't be; but he held up his hand to silence me before I could begin.

"Don't say anything right now. I've got to go

take care of some things. Make yourself at home, think about it, decide what you need to ask, and we'll talk when I get back."

Then he was gone, and I noticed I was feeling good enough to move about a little.

I poked around half-heartedly, discovered that the passage toward the rear of the cave led to a bedroom of sorts. More books, more mysterious tapestries, and an arrangement of blankets and furs similar to the one I'd been waking up in every day.

The other passage was indeed an exit, twisted and convoluted sharply, shielding us perfectly from the elements.

Pouring rain outside, I didn't even approach the mouth of the cave. As far as I could see, there were no lights or roads…not even a trail. No way to tell where Somebody might have gone.

I wondered what was so important that my curious new friend had to do, braving the downpour.

Wandering back to my cozy quarters, I picked a book at random from one of the overflowing shelves. Scratching my head, I swapped it five minutes later for another.

Finally, I found a book that didn't make me feel like a slow child and settled down to read.

* * *

He was back in a few hours, and it didn't strike me until later that his hair and clothes were completely dry.

Immediately, he asked if I was comfortable, if I was hungry. I answered yes on both counts. Slipping into the back room, he emerged momentarily brandishing two fresh salads, one of which he placed before me.

Closing his eyes for a moment, he looked like a vision of peace. Then he opened them and began eating slowly, overchewing each dainty bite he took.

I watched him a moment; then, as he began eating, I dove into mine, one huge mouthful after another, swallowing almost without chewing.

Between bites, I tried to strike up a conversation.

"I was thinking, while you were gone—"

He held up his hand, continued chewing.

"What?" I asked.

He set down his fork, swallowed. "I won't tell you how to eat," he said, "But I will ask that you respect my ways if you would like me to continue respecting yours."

Setting down my fork too, I looked questions at him.

He smiled, nodded for me to ask them.

"What's wrong with the way I eat?" I asked defensively. "I've always had a philosophy when it came to eating and sleeping. They're both timekillers, necessary for survival. Eating is like gassing up your car: you pull up to the pump, put the gas in the car, pay for it and go. The more quickly you get it done, the more time you save. Same with sleep, sleep as few hours as you can and you get more hours in a day. All the talk I always hear about 'eat more slowly, enjoy your food' and 'get your rest, it's good for you' is just a bunch of tripe from a bunch of people who want to eat and sleep their lives away."

Arms folded across my chest, I sat back, prepared to defend my homespun philosophies.

He smiled agreeably, nodded. "Well spoken."

He moved to pick up his fork.

"Do you agree?" I said, exasperated. I wasn't about to let him act as though he wasn't challenging me.

"I don't disagree," he answered simply. "If it works for you, it works for you. It's not the way I see it, it's not the way I choose to do it, but I won't say I'm wrong and you're right. May I eat now?" He reached for his fork again; I waved my hand.

"Hang on," I said. "Do you think your way is better, that it's smarter?"

He shrugged. "Depends on what you want. For me, its better, yes."

"Okay," I growled, "how do you do it, how do you see it?"

"The two things you want to get out of the way as quickly as possible are your two most apparent forms of physical renewal," he said, matter-of-fact. "Personally, in my humble opinion, I feel that the experiences should be treated with respect. I like the idea of being as happy and as healthy as I can be."

I rolled my eyes. "How is me not talking while you happen to be eating going to affect your diet? How could it possibly affect the quality of the food you eat?"

"It won't affect the quality of the food itself," he answered calmly. "It *will*, however, affect the quality of the *experience*. If part of my mind is paying attention to the food and part of my mind is paying attention to you, I'm trying to experience two things at once. Not giving you my full attention while also not giving my food my full attention enables me to have two half-experiences at the same time, but it robs me of the ability to completely savor either one. It's not fair to you, it's not fair to the food, and it's not fair to me. If it's important…" he pushed his plate and fork away, "…we can talk now and eat later. If it can wait, though, I am a bit hungry."

We continued eating then, in silence.

I glanced over from time to time, wondering about him. He did seem completely devoted to each bite, savoring every morsel.

Thinking back, I remembered how it had felt when we talked. I had felt so…*listened to*. I tried to think back, remember when I had felt that way before. I drew a complete blank…not one such memory in a lifetime's storehouse of memories.

I stopped eating and put my fork down resolutely. I stared at him intently, as if looking at him long enough and hard enough would cause me to suddenly understand him somehow.

He pretended not to notice for a minute or two, then put down his fork, wiped his mouth gingerly, and looked me square in the eye.

"All your life you have been surrounded by people who behave as though experience equals wisdom, that because they are older than you they automatically see more clearly. They give advice and the only reason they can come up with for you to listen is 'because I've been there' or 'because I'm older and wiser.'"

Dumbfounded, I gaped at him. He went on:

"There is wisdom to be found in this world, but it is not an incidental by-product of years lived. True wisdom must be sought, it must be chased. You must have a burning desire to attain it, it must be more important than anything. Even yourself sometimes."

He drew himself up proudly. "I am a seeker, I have that burning desire, and *that*…"

Picking his fork up, he pointed it at me. "…that is why I strike you as being so different."

With that, he stood, piled the dinner dishes neatly in one hand, and bade me good night.

* * *

It was after breakfast the next morning that he broached the subject of the deal he had proposed. He had an odd confidence in his voice as he asked his pointed question:

"So, Nobody…you are staying?" It was a question, yes, but it was a statement too.

That kind of annoyed me. I hadn't even been able to completely decide yet. There were too many loose ends I had left behind, and I could feel them unravelling inside me even as we spoke.

"I really don't think I can," I responded. "As far as everyone knows I've disappeared from the face of the Earth. My friends, my parents…they're going to get worried soon, if they're not already."

He cocked an eyebrow at me. "Correct me if I'm wrong, but did you not set out just a few short days ago to end your life? It hardly seems as though you had your friends and family in mind then."

"Well, I *didn't*," I shot back. "I also didn't have to explain myself afterward…I was aiming for the whole 'not having a care in the world' thing. I think that is generally *why* people kill themselves. My car, and everything in it, has been parked for several days right in front of a 'no overnight parking' sign. If it's been towed, I've got to get the money to get it back. If it hasn't, I still need to put gas in it before it will go anywhere. These are things I need to worry about, seeing as how my stay on Earth has been extended." I stopped.

He was shaking his head and rolling his eyes at me.

"What?" I demanded.

He fixed that piercing gaze on me again. "I told you, if you will recall, that everything would be taken care of. It is. If you would like to write to your friends and family to assure them that you are safe, I will make sure it gets to them. However, although I cannot explain why just yet, such measures are unnecessary.

"Also," he added, "your vehicle and your belongings are safe as well. When I promised everything would be taken care of, I did not speak lightly. Nobody," he intoned gravely, "you have been drawn here for a reason. Your whole life has led you to this point. All I'm asking for is the chance to prove it to you."

A chill ran up my spine. It wasn't fear I was feeling, though, it was excitement. His words made me feel a sense of destiny, something I had longed for all my life.

I realized suddenly that I was being uncertain merely for the sake of being uncertain. I didn't care about my car or my things.

I didn't care much about anything at all.

"Okay, I'll do it," I blurted out. I didn't know why, but I felt a huge sense of relief as I said the words.

Somebody just gave me a little smile and nodded, as if he'd been certain of my decision from the beginning.

CHAPTER FOUR

"Splendid," he said, still smiling. "Now I will tell you the one secret that you need to know more than any other, which has been hidden right in front of your face your entire life. You won't know just what I mean because there are a lot of things standing between you and the truth right now. That's what's going to take some time and some energy to work through. The best starting point, I think, though, is to tell you the crucially important thing that is not given nearly enough attention, as best I can: There is only one reason why anyone ever experiences any negative emotion; fear, anger, hate, pain, suffering of any kind, and it's because on some level they don't know this."

He was quiet for a moment, studying me.

I studied him right back. Torn between excitement at the prospect of such knowledge and relief that I knew which door was the exit, I shifted in my seat, cocked an eyebrow at him.

"You are not a human being," he said. "You, and

I, and everyone on this planet, are Spirit. The reason life has never seemed to make sense, the reason you wanted to end your life, is because you were trying to live life as a human being."

He sat back, folded his arms across his chest.

"And you were right. Life is pointless, it makes no sense, *until you learn to live a life of Spirit.*"

I sat there for a moment, silent. He was so friendly, such a nice guy, I hated to offend him.

"Look," I said, "Please don't take it personally or anything. I know you mean well and all, but religion has always seemed to be nothing more than a mental shelter for weak, illogical people to hide behind. I can't live my life by 'because God says so' when it's so clearly a man saying so."

He burst out laughing, clapped his hands like a child. "Well spoken, Nobody, well spoken."

"That's one reaction I never expected from a bible thumper," I sneered. "Now let me tell you what you're going to say next: *my* religion is different, *we're* the chosen ones, *we* know all the right answers, *only we* can save you from Hell and damnation and promise you safe passage into Heaven when you die…" I trailed off, watching Somebody as he watched me. My breath coming fast, I was angry.

He had covered his mouth with one hand. He was trying not to laugh.

I clenched my jaws. "What's so funny?"

He smiled, shook his head. "You are assuming something that is not true, Nobody, then basing your argument on that assumption. You see, my friend, I don't believe in God."

The room was deadly quiet then, as what he'd said sunk in.

Then, in a burst of insight, it struck me what he was doing...he was taunting me, playing with me, talking for no reason than to get me angry and confused. He could tell I had some deep-seated feelings about this, and he just wanted to get me riled up, for the sheer sport of it. I'd done it to people plenty of times before; now I was being made to look like the fool.

Well, no more! I resolved inwardly. *Two can play at this game, Mr. 'Somebody.'*

I had learned, in dealing with people, that its best to act interested, to let people talk. No matter how much you may disagree, it's better not to say so. Just wait, let them talk, and they'll prove themselves hypocrites or idiots or both soon enough. I employed my tactic against him.

Cautiously, I asked, "You don't believe in God?"

"No, I don't," he replied evenly, "I, like you, could never live with myself believing something out of desperation, or because I was told to. I, like you, spent many years as an atheist because I thought there were no options other than blind faith or no faith. Yet, *unlike* you, I discovered a *third* choice, a choice apparently never pursued by the devout religionists or the staunch atheists—"

"Wait, wait!" I interjected. My head was spinning. *How did he know so much about me?* More importantly, I thought, chiding myself, when is he going to start talking nonsense? But he had gotten one thing wrong.

"I never said I was an atheist," I said, drawing myself up proudly. "In fact, I'm not."

He shook his head. "I never said you were an atheist either, Nobody. I said that I, like you, spent many years *as an atheist*. Now you've taken the next step, realizing that you appeared the idiot for assuming there *wasn't* a God as much as others appeared the idiots for assuming there *was*. Now here you are, thinking you are at the end of your journey because you found the honesty and humility to admit to yourself that *you don't know*, because you saw clearly enough to stop calling yourself 'atheist' and start calling yourself 'agnostic.' But you're wrong. That's not the end of your journey, my friend. It's just the beginning."

I gaped at him. How could he *know* that? As I reeled inside, he continued, speaking casually as his words opened me like a scalpel:

"You see, Nobody, by admitting that you don't know, by refusing to pretend that the world is something other than it is, you have revealed yourself. You did not want to die because you felt as though you understood the world and couldn't bear to live in it.

"You wanted to die because you realized you *didn't* understand. You saw that the only people who acted as though they *did* understand were so obviously deceiving themselves that you could feel nothing but disgust for their contradictory philosophies.

"You want the truth, not the hand-me-down lies that are the hallmark of both the religious and the atheist camps. The possibility that the truth could not be known is what drove you to the brink of suicide. But it wasn't actually death that awaited you here, and the part of you that knew that is the part of you that compelled you to come here.

"You came here not to die but to finally learn what

it is to live, to be *Nobody* for a while in your search to become who you truly are, to become something you could be proud of instead of ashamed of."

He sat back, pretending not to notice me picking my jaw up off the floor.

"Who are you?" I whispered intensely.

A grin broke out across his face, lit up the entire room.

"Somebody," he replied, extending his hand. "Nice ta meetcha."

* * *

"Life is suffering." His voice drifted easily across the distance between us. He looked as he had the first time I had seen him, back toward me as he nursed the fire back to health. When I didn't reply, he turned his head until I could see his profile silhouetted by the flames. "Ever hear that one before?"

Decision made, I felt relaxed, at home. Somebody and I were like old pals, completely at ease with each other.

"Yeah, sure, I've heard it, or something like it, plenty of times, my whole life," I answered slowly. "Seems true enough, too. I mean, every time you start to feel like you're getting ahead, like you've finally earned some space to breathe, *Pow!* life knocks you on your ass."

I paused, let my gaze idly wander his simple, perfect home for the hundredth time. I breathed deeply, exhaled slowly, then noticed him watching me. An amused smile was tugging at the corners of his mouth, and it took me a moment to remember what I'd just said.

I flushed, grinned at him. "Well, *usually*, anyways."

"Life is suffering," he repeated, almost to himself, crossing the room and settling comfortably a few feet from me. A solemn look came over his face, and he looked at me. "It's a lie, Nobody. Or more accurately, it's a half-truth, practiced and preached by lazy and irresponsible people throughout history."

I frowned then, because he looked so sad. Shaking my head, I said, "Wait just a minute, didn't that one come straight from the Buddha?"

His eyes flashed at me angrily.

"That's the beauty of language, Nobody. No matter how wise you are, some idiot is bound to take your wisest utterances out of context and twist them into a justification for their pathetic life to continue being pathetic."

Leaning back against the smooth rock wall, he gazed thoughtfully at the ceiling. I knitted my brow together and waited.

"I happen to have it on the highest authority that that was not what the Buddha meant at all. What he *did* mean was that as long as you believe yourself to be a human being, if you must insist that that is who and what you truly are, there is one rule you will never escape: 'Life is suffering.' He tried to clear up that confusion, to explain the other option. Unfortunately, by the time he got around to it, most all his audience had long since quit listening. They had already jumped to their feet and run out into the streets, yelling, 'Life is suffering! The Buddha says so!'"

Laughing, picturing the scene he had so colorfully

painted, I felt myself really starting to like this guy. Something about him put me so very much at ease. I also realized that I was starting to ask him questions for a different reason. I had been challenging him before; now I just wanted to hear what he had to say next.

"Okay, two questions."

He smiled, nodded at me. "Shoot."

"First," I said, leaning forward, "you said you have it on the 'highest authority' that that's what the Buddha meant."

"Yes, I did say that."

"So?"

"So what?"

I rolled my eyes in mock exasperation. "So who's your highest authority? I get the feeling you didn't mean the Dalai Lama."

Standing abruptly, he threw his shoulders back and held his head high. His eyes flashed as he fixed me with a piercing gaze.

"I. AM. GOD." His voice boomed out dramatically. **"THERE. IS. NO. AUTHORITY. HIGHER. THAN. I."**

Then he disintegrated into peals of laughter.

I stared at him, speechless.

Settling back onto the floor, he wiped tears from his eyes. "Nobody, I'm serious." His smile, however, still threatened to turn to laughter. "I am God, manifested here for the sheer fun of having an experience in physicality. How much higher of an authority could there be?" He sobered about mid-sentence, and I suppose I did too.

"So what's so special about you?" I was starting to sound petulant again. "If you're God manifested in physical form, aren't *I* God manifested in physical form as well?"

The fire leapt up high just then, crackled and snapped explosively. I jumped, but Somebody just watched me calmly. The fire seemed to burn in his eyes as well, as he answered:

"Of *course* you are God manifested in physical form. The thing that makes me special is that I *know* it. I feel it, every moment, in every cell of my being. I know the answer to every question you ask because I asked them all myself, and couldn't rest until I'd found answers. I didn't make up convenient answers to fit my narrow perspective, despite the truth. I pursued the highest perspective I could, in spite of myself. *That* is what imbues me with the highest authority; *that* is why my words always have the ring of truth."

"Ask a question…" I murmured.

"Get an answer!" He winked conspiratorially at me. "And speaking of questions…" he looked at me expectantly.

I blinked. "What?"

Rolling his eyes, he mocked me. "Your other question, my curious new friend. You did say there were two."

"Oh! Right." I remembered now. "You said the Buddha tried to clear that up, to explain 'the other option.'"

He was nodding. "So what's 'the other option,' right?"

"So what's the other option?" I echoed.

He moved to tend the fire, but stopped as I held up my hand. Rising, I fetched his hand axe and deftly chopped a round of larch into perfect quarters. Turning to stir the coals, I caught a look of calm satisfaction on his face. I turned away to hide my own.

Stacking the fresh wood expertly, I listened to his answer.

"The other option is really the only option. Believing that you are a human being is believing a lie, and living as a human being is living a lie. *Knowing* that you are Spirit causes you to live a life of Spirit. It causes you to know every moment of every day that there is no such thing as suffering, or tragedy, or misfortune. It causes you to know complete *peace*, complete *trust*, complete *happiness*. These are words that you have heard repeatedly throughout your life, whose true meaning you have yet to discover. You have heard people who never bothered to discover what these words meant throwing them about casually; but it is their intention that makes them meaningless, not the words themselves."

Flames leaping high, I settled in front of him and leaned against my tree stump/nightstand, completely at ease.

"You don't much care for people, do you?" I asked. His words sounded disgusted, but the tone of his voice held no bitterness, no contempt. I wondered at that.

"I love people." He spoke gently, quietly, gazing into the flames. "Everyone plays their roles perfectly, never skipping a beat. There is no such thing as evil, and therefore nothing worth hating."

Those eyes turned to me again, and I fell into their depths. I was hypnotized, each word he spoke burning itself into my mind.

"The only folly of the common man, Nobody, the true 'original sin,' is nothing more than a simple mistake in phrasing... You see, we are not human beings, we are simply *being human*, and only for a drop in the ocean of time. Once you realize that, and it's never a moment too soon, you are free to begin living life as it is meant to be lived."

A comfortable silence drew itself out then, calm descending like a blanket.

He looked sideways at me, after a long moment. "Does that, uh, answer your question?"

* * *

"What about handicapped people?" It occurred to me, next day. "What about people born blind, or even worse, blinded by an accident? What about the people being born every day with no chance of surviving the week for lack of food or shelter? They suffer inevitably, no matter what they believe. What about them?"

We had stepped outside, and the day was glorious. Everything looked so alive, colors so bright. Somebody was basking in it, head tilted back as the sunlight bathed his face. It took him a moment to answer.

"Ah, the fortunate," he whispered. "How to explain?"

Eyes closed, face still toward the sun, he spoke so softly I had to lean closer to hear.

"That's a very good question, also a very human question. The answer only makes sense if you stop pretending that you are a human being. Can you do that, just for a moment?" He opened his eyes, turned to look at me.

I nodded. "I'll try."

"Good enough." He turned back toward the sun, closed his eyes again.

"Humans call these people unfortunate. Once again, they've got it backwards. The blind man is prompted all the more to discover his true nature, to see the light of his *being* behind the darkness of his eyes. His choice leads him to either exclaim his life to be a beautiful, wonderful thing or to wallow in the very human experience of self-pity.

"The starving man is even more fortunate, for him it is very much do or die: either recognize that you are Spirit, that the thought of Spirit starving is a ridiculous one at best, or suffer wretched painful death as a human being."

He turned again from the sun, sat on a bed of grass, patted the ground beside him.

I sat. "So what about people with severe psychological or physical disorders, people who can't be reached at all, no matter how wise your words?" I had worked with people like that, could never answer the question: Why?

"What has struck you about these people, Nobody? What impression have you walked away with from your experience with what you consider severely handicapped people?"

I thought about that. "Honestly?"

He picked a grass stem from the ground, chewed it. "No, lie to me." The grass flew at me, bounced harmlessly off my arm. "Of course, honestly."

The stem shot right back at him, and our little war was over.

"I remember working with a few people, they

couldn't talk, couldn't understand a word you said. I remember wondering why they smiled virtually nonstop, why they'd laugh and clap their hands at the slightest things…"

He was watching me closely. "Go on."

Looking away, I said, "I remember thinking 'why do you get to be all ecstatic all the time, and not me?' I resented them for it, came to the conclusion that ignorance is indeed bliss; the less intelligent you are, the more happy you get to be. I decided I liked to be smart and miserable more than I'd like to be stupid and happy."

A long silence followed, me amazed at my own candid honesty, Somebody looking deep in thought at my side.

I reached to pick another grass stem, hit him square in the forehead with it. "Well?"

"Some people call these people highly advanced souls, spending a completely unselfish life on Earth for the sake of helping those around them. Yet we are all 'highly advanced,' we are all Masters, we are all pure Spirit pretending it doesn't know this, hasn't felt that, knows everything, knows nothing, is tall, is slim, is pretty, is fat, is mean, is miserable, is happy—"

"I get it already!" I laughed. "So some people are here just to help others learn what they need to learn, to accomplish what they're here for? That does sound pretty unselfish, pretty 'highly advanced.'"

"Well, it's not," he retorted. "Unselfishness is yet another lie that you've got to unlearn."

"Waitjustaminute!" That bothered me, didn't quite fit right. I shifted in my grassy seat to turn and look at him square. "Even *I* know, deep down inside, that one of the most wonderful and uplifting experiences you can have is helping someone who is incapable of helping themselves."

He cocked an eyebrow, leaned closer. "Are you telling me that you have experienced joy, wonder, even exhilaration helping someone do something they were pretending not to be able to do themselves?"

"No," I interjected quickly. "They *weren't* pretending! I'm talking about people with Alzheimer's, with Cerebral Palsy, with—"

He was watching me again, quietly amused. "Nobody, if you could live a life with severe limitations that gave hundreds of people hundreds of thousands of opportunities to feel the exhilaration that you felt helping those people, can you imagine how exhilarating that would be? Could you really call yourself selfless, knowing that without you pretending your handicaps those people would never know what it is to feel that?

"It takes one damned selfish person to put so much time and energy into helping others to learn about themselves, to dedicate an entire life to offering such an opportunity to others. There is joy to be found in helping others; but if you believe your motive to be selflessness, then you are lying to yourself. If you are not seeking a greater degree of happiness, consciously, every time you extend a helping hand to your neighbor, then your actions are self-destructive. You would be better off not trying to help them at all, and so would they."

A bird chirped. Trees swayed in the breeze. The sun dipped behind a cloud, only to reappear a moment later. And none of it seemed quite real. Something about being around him, everything just looked so…different.

I deliberately chose the biggest, heaviest, meanest looking blade of grass I could find. I hefted the thing like a javelin. Threw it.

It stuck in his hair. He feigned irritation as he brushed it away.

"Bastard!" I hissed playfully.

"Whatever did I do?" he asked innocently, spreading his hands.

"I told you. I always knew there were two choices: either I could be smart and miserable, or I could be dumb and happy."

He arched his eyebrows. "And…"

"*And*…you're smart. You're probably…no, you're *definitely* the smartest person I've ever met. You're also the happiest person I've ever met. You just blew my theory all to hell…*Bastard*."

He threw his head back then, and he laughed. He laughed until I couldn't help but join in.

And there we sat, for I don't how long, side by side, laughing like two complete madmen caught up in the bliss of madness.

Yet I was beginning to feel sane for the first time in my life.

CHAPTER FIVE

My brow was furrowed in concentration. There was something here I needed to understand.

"So you're saying…" I drew my words out carefully, as I was learning to do with him "…you're saying that I *chose* to be six foot tall, I *chose* my blonde hair and blue eyes, I *chose* my mother, *chose* my father, *chose* my sister, *chose* my talents and even *chose* my hang-ups…?" It sounded incredible to me, especially if it were true.

He was exasperated. He paced in front of the fire, casting me in and out of his shadow. He had the manner of an impatient professor astounded that his most brilliant student couldn't add one and one and arrive successfully at two.

(I was honestly trying.)

"I mean, Jesus, dude!" I frowned fiercely at him. "I decided I wanted *that particular childhood?!* I wouldn't wish that on my worst enemy!"

"Sum up your life for me in a few short sentences, Nobody."

It was such a different track, I just did it:

"I hated being a kid. I always wanted my own life, my own place, my own thing, y'know?" He nodded. "I hated my parents because they were my parents, there to constantly remind me that I wasn't my own person yet."

He yawned, and I talked faster.

"Then I got out on my own only to realize I didn't have a 'thing.' I was just getting by, like everyone else, and the treadmill felt exhausting from the moment I first set foot on it."

I sighed. "Now I've got some strange dude telling me that I've got it all wrong and something about what he says sounds so right and I just don't know what to think."

He clasped his hands solemnly behind his back, peered at me through the leaping shadows. "And do you think that you'd have been ready to hear your very first truths from this 'strange dude' if it had unfolded any other way?"

I blinked. "Probably not."

"And doesn't this moment shine forth beautifully due only to the light shed on it by every moment that came before it?"

I had to smile. "Yeah, I suppose it does."

"And doesn't it strike you right now just how perfect and wonderful is this Universe you have called forth?"

There were tears in my eyes. "Hey, Somebody." Our eyes met. "Yeah?"

"Thanks."

He smiled. "Anytime."

* * *

I was lying down. He'd bade me goodnight not five minutes earlier.

"You awake?" I hollered it just loud enough to wake him up if he was already asleep.

Lumbering out, he paused just long enough to stir the coals of the fire, then came to sit at the edge of my bed.

"Why don't I remember? Why for the life of me can't I remember deciding that my life was going to be set up just so, that it would unfold a certain way and lead me invariably to what I needed to learn just when I needed to learn it?"

I glanced at him, went on:

"I mean, it makes sense, that I chose this path, these challenges. I'll buy that." I shook my head. "But why can't I *remember* choosing it?"

He had a wooden chessboard, an ornate stand and board that were one piece, hand-carved in painstakingly meticulous detail. Each character was lovingly crafted, queens standing a majestic eight inches high. He'd carved half of them from birch, the other half from larch.

I'd challenged him to a game once. He beat me cold.

I'd tried again a couple days later, more careful this time. He defused my offense completely, annihilated my defense utterly. Within fifteen, maybe twenty moves.

The board had sat untouched since. Now he maneuvered it across the room to settle it squarely between us.

Birch on my side of the board, it was his move nonetheless.

He chose a pawn from my side. "Imagine yourself a pawn…" he murmured.

"Hang on," I interrupted. "As long as we're imagining…"

Dropping the pawn, he grasped the king instead. "Better, Your Majesty?"

I smiled, shook my head. I picked up a knight and tossed it at him. He snatched it from the air and set the king down.

"Imagine yourself a *knight*," he said sarcastically.

I grinned.

"Imagine," he continued, "being able to *be* the knight, not the piece but the man. See yourself living that life, one moment to the next, within certain restrictions and with certain thoughts and hopes and dreams and abilities that are completely unique to you."

I closed my eyes to see it better.

"Play out a whole chess game, beginning to end, a lifetime long. See yourself surrounded by people, not pieces, all living out their own lives. Kings and queens, rooks and bishops."

My eyes flashed open. "And knights." He sighed. "And knights."

I shut my eyes again.

"Now and then you are called upon to fulfill some duty that only you can perform, something vitally important to the survival of your community. Like two spaces this way and one that."

I ignored his sarcasm. I was really into it. "See it?" he asked me softly.

"Mm-hmm…" I murmured.

"Now try and watch your queen slaughtered while you stand idle."

I frowned. No big deal, though; the rare miracle can bring her back. I told him so.

"Now the rooks."

"Both of them?"

"Both of them."

"Well, aside from the fact that they're my second favorite piece to attack with, no major problem. Unless I'm not doing comparable damage to my enemy." I opened my eyes long enough to look the question at him.

He assured me I was keeping up.

Down the list we went, him casually killing off my bishops and pawns and me gleefully showing no remorse whatsoever for my fellow fallen Birchians. I was getting quite concerned about the outcome of the game, but I just couldn't bring myself to cry over a chess piece.

It was down to the king and I when it struck me. "It's still just a game, though. Kill us both off and we reincarnate a moment later. No blood; no fuss, no muss." My eyes were wide open.

He nodded.

"Now do it all over," he said. "Only this time make one of the rules of the game that you have to *forget it's a game.*"

I was imagining again behind my eyelids. A light was beginning to dawn.

"Now you find yourself waking for all you know for the first time ever onto a board whose rules you don't automatically get to understand. You learn slowly that you can move this way and that but not that way and this."

I saw my queen slaughtered again, only I didn't know she could be brought miraculously back to life; I'd never seen such a thing. My beloved queen was lost forever. And I wanted to cry.

I knew of no worthwhile goal, no point to this life, knew not how to win or lose.

The only thing I knew for sure was that death was coming.

I learned that as I watched my cherished rooks, men with hopes and dreams and fears and fantasies; as I watched him end their one chance at leading long and potentially fulfilling lives. Death came as swiftly and as mercilessly for them as it had for my queen, as I knew it would soon come for me.

I stopped his killing spree before I developed abandonment issues.

"Alright, so we forget. We forget so that we can take it seriously, live it to the hilt; not just play a part, but be the part we're playing. Have thoughts and dreams and fears and fantasies, all our own. And believe it."

"Because it's true," he said.

"But it's not," I responded, a frown creasing my forehead.

"Exactly." He beamed at me.

CHAPTER SIX

The river flowed. Over rocks, through trees… restlessly yet peacefully, the river flowed.

Somebody had awakened before I had, was gone before I even began to stir. I chuckled at the thought of the ease with which we had fallen into a comfortable routine. Normally I woke to find him either gone or reading quietly so as to avoid disturbing my sleep.

And normally, when I awoke to find him gone, I lounged about until he returned. The birdsong had drawn me out this morning, though, and I was glad for it. It was peaceful, it was beautiful, the kind of day that pulls you right out of yourself.

My thoughts raged noisily in my mind.

I wondered why I wasn't bothered by all that I was neglecting, all that I had left behind. The week he had asked me to commit to had long since gone…someone else's distant past. Our long talks, even our long comfortable silences, were already becoming my favorite memories. They seemed to be the most *real* memories I had, like I was slowly waking from a long and terrible nightmare.

It still seemed somehow unreal, like I couldn't accept that the nightmare wasn't the way things were supposed to be. It seemed to be true, it seemed so right that maybe Somebody was the sanest person I had ever met. Yet…and that was just it. Whenever I tried to see some flaw in the picture he was painting, some weak point in the outrageous things he said, I just couldn't. That had never happened to me before, with *anyone*.

The more he spoke, the more I wanted to hear. More than anything, I just wanted to hear more, to understand more.

Hands in my pockets, I walked along the river's edge. I kicked absently at a rock, my attention turned inward to my racing mind.

"But *why*?" I asked suddenly, aloud. "Why would we even want to do this in the first place?"

"Because it's fun."

I jumped, whirled toward him. I had almost walked right by him.

Somebody sat comfortably amidst bright foliage, grass flattened under him as he contemplated the river.

He was glowing.

I did a double-take, looked more closely. No, he wasn't really *glowing*, was he? It had to be the way the sun…

Looking closely, I fell into him. I was swept suddenly with love for this man, for this river, for this Universe, for this life…

Tears streamed unnoticed down my cheeks. I held my hands to my face in wonder. Not my hands, not my face…

I laughed.

Then I sobbed, fell to my knees.

Rolling on the ground, my body shook with laughter, then with sobs, then with laughter again.

He never moved.

The intensity of the emotion, the experience, it gripped me and then passed, ebbed and then flowed, again and again.

I cried for it to stop, for it to never stop. Finally, it passed, and I lay on the ground, panting. My head rolled to the side, my eyes found his.

"What in the hell was *that*?!"

He finally broke his solemn posture, laughed out loud, cleared his throat.

Tears shone in his eyes.

"That, Nobody, is what I live with every moment of every day." He spoke as I stood and wiped the tears from my face and the grass from my jeans. "That is why when you ask why on Earth we would ever come here, ever choose to live a life or a thousand or a billion lives as a human being, one at a time or all at the same time…"

He looked up at me.

I had paused, hand in the air over my pant leg, midswipe.

He smiled.

"That is why I cannot see why you cannot see that you are here to have fun."

"That…" I waved my hand in the direction of my recent ecstatic convulsions, "…that was not fun."

He frowned. "No?"

"That was incredible! That made fun look dull! That was, that was…" I reached.

"That was the barest glimpse of man's natural

state; that was all the bliss you can handle right now without flying apart in a million different directions."

"Doesn't sound so bad," I mused. "But still, why the pain? Why not just forego all the 'human suffering' rigamarole and get right to the 'flying apart in a million different directions?'"

He stood, started walking back the way I had come. I fell into step beside him.

"You are a human being, Nobody?"

"I'm starting to wonder…"

"Good," he said firmly. "Because seeing yourself as human is the best way to ensure that you will live a reality of pain and torment whose only point is eventual release."

"And if I see myself as Spirit…?"

Nodding, he said, "…and if you learn to see *through the eyes* of Spirit, you will see that you are Divinity, manifesting as Spirit, which is in turn manifesting as a human being, who is pretending that there is such a thing as soulwrenching, heartbreaking pain."

"Now hang on," I grimaced. "I've *felt* that soul-wrenching, heartbreaking pain you so flippantly dismiss. I was going to kill myself, remember?"

"And where would that have gotten you?"

"Not Hell, I know that now." I glanced at him. "Right?"

He stopped walking, and we stood there and stared at each other a moment.

"Ever see a child who didn't know any better do something that from your broader and more experienced perspective seemed like an obviously bad decision?" He looked straight into my eyes.

"Yeah, sure."

"Ever feel inclined to start a huge fire and cast them into it, wishing only that you could somehow make the punishment last an eternity?"

I sighed. "God, no."

"And do you somehow really think that God or Goddess or whatever symbol or shape you need is such a hateful being or force that he or she or it would condemn you to eternal pain and suffering for being a dumb kid occasionally?"

"So I'd have been Spirit again, whole and undamaged despite how I felt." I raised an eyebrow. "Right?"

"You were driven by how you felt to experience yourself as you truly are by any means necessary." As he walked away, he called over his shoulder, "The Universe just thought I'd be a little less messy of an option."

I ran a few steps, slowed beside him. "But *why the pain*? I feel better about my life right now than I ever have, but I'm still scared and confused and really quite angry that nobody ever told me this stuff before. Why don't I just live the wonder and excitement and benevolence of what you say is true?"

Halting again, he faced me.

I turned to him, and we stood a foot apart.

Lightning-fast, his foot flashed out and stomped mine, hard.

Then he turned and walked away.

I plopped down on the grass and clutched my throbbing foot.

"Hey!" I yelled after him.

He stopped, turned.

"Yes?"

I glared at him.

"What the hell did you do that for?"

His voice was soft, but it carried on the breeze:

"Before I stomped on your foot, you were all but completely unaware of it. When I stomped on it you once again became aware of your precious foot. When it feels better in a few minutes you will gaze with great appreciation on the very thing that you were but a moment ago taking completely for granted."

He spun on his heel and strode purposefully up the river's edge.

It hurt for a minute, it really did, so much I didn't want to walk on it.

I sat, thinking on what he'd said, and when I finally got up and walked there was a spring in my step that hadn't been there a minute ago.

* * *

Candles cast a dim glow over Somebody's shadowy form.

He leaned forward, into the light.

"This is how our deepest desires get our attention."

I didn't say a word, just waited.

"First they whisper in our ear, give us pleasant daydreams, possibilities, future memories, the next step in the highest direction.

"Then, if they are ignored, they tap us on the shoulder, talk a bit louder, a bit more forcefully. Every song on the radio reminds you of what you're missing, every television broadcast, newspaper headlines jump out at you, saying something to you that you know they're not saying to anyone else.

"If you *still* don't listen, *still* refuse to change course, your desires, your lessons will begin to shout in your ear, to box you around a little. Things get tougher, a good day is a rare day, that sort of thing."

He paused, shook his head, contemplated a candle.

"Now things get ugly. If you continue to ignore and to thwart your own deepest desires, no matter how unhappy you become, no matter how difficult life becomes, you leave the Universe no other option."

His voice grew low and ominous.

"After whispering, after shouting, after tripping you up and still being trampled underfoot, your deepest desires choose the only option you have left them with. Your legs get broken. Your Spirit gets broken. Your mind gets broken. You will lie there on your back, empty and hollow and lifeless, until you die or learn your lesson and discover and pursue at all cost your deepest desires, your next highest truth."

My mind raced. "Figuratively, right?"

"Yes, of course," he answered blithely. "Like you were going to figuratively kill yourself."

"Point taken. But—"

"Nobody." I shut up. "Everyone has deep desires, things they want to do here on Earth, for whatever reason. We have long since decided most of these things on a deeper level, and we must learn to access these levels within ourselves if we are to discover and manifest our own highest potential."

"Because it's fun," I clarified. He nodded. "But when we don't…?"

"When we don't, we get our legs broken. We get into terrible accidents, contract lethal diseases, we force ourselves into a do-or-die decision. Then we try to look at these symptoms of a lacking Spiritual life the same way we looked at everything else, the whispering and the shoulder-tapping. If we keep seeing from the flawed and incomplete perspective of a human being, we oblige ourselves by dying the death of a human being. It doesn't matter how long said death takes, when you die without bothering to discover who and what you truly are, you have died without ever knowing what it means to live."

Finally, a smile broke out across his face. "If, however, we can lift ourselves high enough to even *glimpse* the fact that everything has its source in Spirit, that life, as a rule, celebrates life…well. Then we get to find our highest and deepest desires, to celebrate and fulfill them, to learn to listen to the whispers of wisdom, to rush to heed a tap on the shoulder, to never again resort to breaking our own legs just to discover how to walk. We get to learn that death is an illusion, that the idea itself is absolutely preposterous."

"Sounds nice," I admitted.

He rolled his eyes.

CHAPTER SEVEN

"So there *is* such a thing as Fate?" I'd always wanted it, that sense of a higher purpose. For the first time, I felt I could dare to hope such things were true. "You believe that, don't you?"

Somebody warmed his hands by the open fire.

"Be careful," he cautioned me. "You don't want to hear what people believe, you want to know what they've discovered. All too often people believe something to avoid the responsibility of having to discover a higher truth. What I believe is irrelevant. What I've discovered is astounding."

"Why can't I even ask a question right?!" I sputtered, exasperated.

"It's your perspective, friend," he chuckled. "It will kill you if you don't change it."

He ran his fingers through his hair.

"Maybe it's just me, but I prefer *Destiny*."

I closed my eyes, as I found myself doing more and more often as he spoke.

"Fate always sounds like doom to me. 'He was

Fated to die, Fate put that poor girl in a wheelchair, accept your Fate.'" He made a gagging sound.

"Now a Destiny, yes! A Destiny is something that you must fulfill! If you came to this wonderful little planet to do something truly beautiful, truly significant (and we all did), then *that* is your Destiny, to be discovered and fulfilled the very best you possibly can."

I opened my eyes. "Bravo," I murmured.

He grinned slyly. "Want me to tell you what your next question is?"

"What?"

Then, on cue, I said it with him:

"So what's my Destiny?"

We smiled at each other.

"So?" I pressed him.

He shrugged.

"You don't know?"

He shrugged again.

"Suddenly you can't talk? You bubble over all day with intelligence and happiness and optimism and you've got not one word to say about the one thing I came here to do?" I was kidding, yes; but I was a little hurt, too.

That gentle smile lighted his face, as he explained: "Listen, it's not 'one thing.' You didn't come here to accomplish some one isolated thing and then die. Yes, you were born to do something, to do many things. But they are things you must discover, it is a path you must walk as it unfolds. Even if I told you the one thing you will enjoy more than anything in the world it wouldn't help. It may even stunt it, put pressure on you that you haven't yet learned to channel properly. Learn first and foremost that you are Spirit. The rest will come to you."

"So you know?"

He winced. "Yeah. I'm a big fan, actually."

I eyed him suspiciously, and we both laughed.

Opening my mouth to press him further, I caught the look in his eye.

He was reading my mind again, shaking his head solemnly.

"Goodnight, Nobody."

CHAPTER EIGHT

Our walks by the river became a daily routine as the weather improved. The rising temperatures, the frequency with which we were beginning to see the sun, made me wonder just how long I had been here with Somebody. One does not begin to see the sun in the Puget Sound area until winter has begun to loosen its grip.

I had quit my job December thirty-first. It hadn't been any more than two weeks into the new year that I had set out on this unintentional adventure.

Months had passed since I had become "Nobody." Not weeks, *months*.

It seemed like days.

As I thought about it, I realized I didn't want to leave.

I thought of how I was constantly astounded anew by this man. It wasn't just the things he said, it was how *genuine* he was. I had never known how much I missed that until I finally found it, nor how deeply I had missed what it was that I felt because of it:

Respect. I'd used the word before, never realizing how terribly I had abused it. Now, looking at him lost in thought, I felt it well up within me, overflow in the form of tears from my eyes.

His glance caught me looking. As always, he knew what I was thinking, and he smiled. Removing his shoes, he wiggled his toes and settled his feet in the cold water.

"Being human is such fun," he said quietly, "when you know that's what you're doing, and why."

We had sat in silence for several minutes as the river soothed my soul. His voice soothed it all the more.

"It's such a leap you're trying to make here." His brow furrowed. "*Going* to make here."

"I think I'm doing a lot better," I said, a little defensive. "I mean, so much makes sense now. And sometimes I feel it…y'know, *feel* the Universe ticking away flawlessly all around me."

"Yes, yes, I know, and that's good," he answered. "But that's just the beginning of the beginning, and it slips away as unbidden as it comes, doesn't it?"

Of course he was right. My earnest glance was enough to keep him talking.

"See, you're beginning to see finally," as he spoke, he stood, arms aloft to the sky, "that you are *everything*, that everything is an individual expression of the same thing."

"Spirit," I whispered, solemn.

"Spirit, Energy, Love, God, Goddess, the Universe, whatever," he smiled.

"For so long you experienced the limited reality of being a tiny speck of consciousness in a big baffling Universe."

Suddenly he held a magnifying glass in one hand, waved my look of astonishment away with the other.

"You concentrated all this desire…"

He waved vaguely at the sky.

"…to a single point of consciousness…"

He indicated the magnifying glass, holding it so as to create a fine beam of light.

"…because when you were that…"

Again at the sky.

"…you couldn't do *this*."

He pointed at the magnifying glass with a flourish.

I looked at him, doing my best to look wise and understanding.

"Look," he said decisively. "The point is this: it's good that you picked this particular model," he indicated my body, "with its eyes and ears and emotions and thoughts, but *that is not what you are*. You may do all in your power to *express* who you are through this particular instrument, but if you see yourself as the instrument your perception will cause you no end of pain and frustration.

"If, however," he turned that full-on burning gaze my way, and I listened closely, "*If*, however, you can feel in every cell of your being, every moment of every day that you are everything, that everything is nothing less than perfection itself…" he sighed. "If you can discover the way in which this instrument you created was specifically designed to be used, if you can be aware of this," he held up the magnifying glass, "without ever losing sight of this," he gestured gloriously at the sky, "well, then…"

I frowned, because I wanted to cry. But I didn't want to cry, I wanted to *be* there.

"How?" I whispered.

I pretended not to notice the disappearance of the magnifying glass.

"More importantly, *when*?" I asked.

"When you do," he answered firmly. "You know now that everything makes sense, that everything happens for a reason and that there is indeed a life here on Earth for you that is indeed worth living. Let's call that a good start."

I thought about that for the rest of the day. It was hard to think back, just a couple months, to how I had felt, what I'd been thinking. Here I was, happier and clearer than I'd ever been in my life… and I just wanted more.

Nothing had ever grabbed my attention so completely, so thoroughly; nothing had been so worthy of pursuit as this thing I felt welling up from within me.

I cried myself to sleep that night, for the first time in my life so happy I couldn't contain it.

And I slept like a baby.

* * *

The inevitable rainy day came, and I found myself lounging in the calm shelter of the cave with Somebody.

He had lit every candle and a blazing fire. The warmth and the glow were hypnotic, lulling.

It made it easier to believe what was happening.

Eyes closed, I was laid back, comfortable. One hand was face up, fingers splayed but relaxed.

One after another, Somebody was placing objects on my open palm.

"Tell me what you feel."

I'm young, but I've done my share of hard physical labor. Through the rough thickness of my hands, I could discern nothing but lightness. Not even a shape.

"Powerful, fast," the words came almost unbidden, "ferocious yet noble. Mmm…" Good feeling, that; but the object was suddenly removed, another put in its place.

"Wholeness realized," I murmured. "Perfection through patience."

Again, the object was replaced.

"Courageous, fearless, strong, *so* strong."

He took it gently from my hand, told me I could open my eyes now.

Chills ran up my spine as he revealed them, one at a time.

First, the eagle's claw; powerful, fast, ferocious and noble.

Next came a beautiful rounded stone, decades spent rolling along the river's bottom to arrive finally at the very shape he held in his hand.

And finally, the bear claw, with its courage and fearless strength.

Racking my brain, frowning, I tried to explain:

"Well, it could be my subconscious, picking up subtleties my conscious mind overlooked as to the shape of the thing in my hand."

He nodded solemnly. "Could be."

"Could be my mind picking up your thoughts," I suggested. "I know it sounds far out to some people, but I see it happen all the time."

He nodded again. "Could be that."

"Or that we see things with our eyes closed all the time." I didn't mean it to come out that way, but he laughed and nodded.

He sighed then. "Could be that you and everyone and everything are all individual parts of the same whole and when you touch a place inside you where you know that's true it enables you to see the whole *and* the parts all the more clearly."

"Hmph." I nodded grudgingly. "Could be."

"I took your normal senses away, and you immediately shifted to another source of input," he said excitedly. "You didn't scoff and you didn't turn away, you just went with it. That's how you grow, not by guessing at what may be but by searching for what is."

"By any means necessary," I whispered.

"By all means available to you," he chided me gently. "This can be a trying struggle, but why not make it a grand adventure?

"Everything is an expression of you, and you are free to express anything through that." His voice captivated me. "You must become aware of that to make your life magickal. The more aware of it you become, the more magickal your life becomes."

He gestured at the items he had laid in my palm. "You think that's magick?"

I shrugged.

Casually, he waved his arm, and a bank of candles blew out across the room.

I gaped.

"You think that's magick?"

Watching my face, he smiled as the candles relit, one by one.

His voice was low, dangerous. "You think that's magick?"

"Yeah, sure, I guess so…" I stammered, amazed.

"That is the careful manipulation of subtle energies slightly beyond your present range of comprehension," he shrugged, offhandedly.

He stepped forward, placed his hand over my heart.

"This is *magick*," he murmured.

My heart exploded outward in all directions. My entire world blew apart in an instant, and it was ecstasy.

I was everything and everything was perfect and LOVE and JOY and HAPPINESS washed over me and through me and I drowned in it blissfully and…

…And it was a good thing I was lying down.

He removed his hand and I lay there, breathing in gasps.

Between breaths, I managed to gasp, "Now. that. is. magick."

CHAPTER NINE

Rain makes one especially thoughtful, it seems. It continued another day, and wet and cold outside made us appreciate all the more the warmth and dryness of the cave.

We each read, him a deathly-dull looking book with numerous charts and graphs, me an "excellent read" suggested by my friend.

It was a good book, too, but his presence in the room was a guarantee that neither of us would be reading long.

He was already looking up expectantly when I raised my head to speak up.

I stopped my thought, though, shifted tracks.

"How do you do that?"

He smiled innocently. "Do what?"

"How do you know what I'm going to do before I do it, what I'm going to say before I say it?"

He just smiled.

"And for that matter, how did you make those candles go out and relight, how do you make things appear and disappear, how is it that you never get wet when you go outside no matter how hard it's raining and—"

He was laughing now. I was too, but I went on:

"*And*, probably most *importantly*…"

He stopped laughing, looked at me solemnly.

"How is it that I feel so very clear, so utterly happy, so confident and excited when I'm around you?" I asked quietly.

"It's not me, Nobody, it's you," he answered, shaking his head.

"Well, naturally." I rolled my eyes in good-natured sarcasm.

"You're falling in love with life," he said simply, and I nodded.

"Now, do you want the parlor tricks, or do you want unbridled happiness?"

I frowned. "Can't I have both?"

"Humor me."

"Okay." I shrugged. "Easy. Unbridled happiness."

"Good," he answered firmly. "Unbridled happiness is born of your burgeoning new perspective, and once you feel that coursing through you every moment, magick will be everywhere. As a happy by-product."

On cue, the sun shone its rare ray that hit the rocks just right to light up the cave.

I dashed outside, shocked and at the same time completely unsurprised: There was not a cloud in the sky.

A chill ran up my spine.

"The weather, too?!" I hollered loud enough so he would hear me inside the cave.

I needn't have bothered. Somebody stood beside me, shoulders shaking with silent laughter.

Suddenly, I remembered what I'd meant to ask him.

"Somebody," I murmured, "do you pray?"

"My life is a prayer," he answered simply.

My brow furrowed. "Is that a yes?"

Chuckling, he asked, "Do you mean do I set aside time to get on my knees and close my eyes and acknowledge and give thanks to my Creator, or to ask for guidance in finding and pursuing my next highest truth?"

"Yeah, that."

"Yes, I do, when I feel compelled to do so."

I snapped my fingers in triumph. "So you *do* believe in God! Admit it!"

He burst out laughing. "No, my friend, I will admit no such thing."

I shook my head at him.

Still laughing, he said, "I do not *believe* in God. If I did, my prayers would be a pointless waste of time. I do not believe in God, the entity that is some authority figure who created me on a whim and may at any moment destroy me on a similar whim.

"I *know* God, intimately and deeply: I know God as the incredible process of which I am a part; and in being a part, I am the whole. I know it and I feel it, and there is nothing greater than that in the whole of the human experience.

"If I had to believe, it would be because I did not know. And believing is a tribute unworthy of God, when knowing is so available to us."

"Is it?!" I snapped. "If this is so easy, if this is so important, then why are you the first person I've ever met who is where you are, who knows what you know? Why aren't people screaming this from the tops of the highest mountains? Why don't I know at least a few people who live like you do? Are they all secretly living out their lives in caves in the middle of nowhere?"

An amused smile lit up his face as he held up his hand to halt my ranting.

"We all know this in the deepest levels of our beings, Nobody, and there are indeed plenty of people who have visited and acknowledged these levels. There are even a good handful of people who live constantly on levels that I haven't even glimpsed yet.

"And no, they don't all live in caves in the middle of nowhere. I don't even live here, I just came here to meet you."

He sighed. "As for screaming from the highest mountaintop, well…people don't want to hear the truth until they've suffered so much and so deeply that they can't take living a lie any more. Even then the stubborn ones don't listen, they just die and proceed on to wherever they decide to go next."

He looked at me sharply.

"Hey!" I protested. "I was listening, more and more! I was miserable, and I knew it, and I hungered for an explanation, some way it all made sense. Hell, I even prayed, I was so desperate. I was ashamed of myself when I did, felt weak and pitiful and…"

I trailed off. A tear slipped from my left eye, unnoticed.

When I spoke again, it was in a whisper, and behind that whisper was awe: "I hadn't prayed since I was a little kid. I was a proud atheist by the time I was twelve, and an even prouder agnostic by sixteen. I spent my fair share of time wondering if there was a God; I debated any believer happily about it, but pray?" I shook my head. "No way."

Somebody was watching me, smiling softly. I was miles away, my eyes staring off into the distance of the past.

I could hear my own voice from far away, distant like a narrator: "I honestly didn't know why I had come out here until I got here. I'd been sleeping in the back of my car and I had a horrible nightmare. I knew I was about to die and it scared the shit out of me."

My voice was low and slow as I relived the moment in my mind, remembering the details I had forgotten until now.

"But it was comforting at the same time. It was over, all of it. Finally… When I woke up I was scared like never before. Disappointed, too. But mostly scared." I shuddered. "*Terrified*. Then I prayed. If you had asked me yesterday what I'd done after that nightmare I'd have said I just fell back to sleep." I blinked slowly, shook my head. "But I didn't. I prayed. I prayed fervently, with all my heart.

"I asked God, if there was such a thing, if he or she or it happened to be there and happened to be listening, to prove to me that life was worth living… that it wasn't just one year after the next of dull and painful routine. A meaningless life followed by a meaningless death was all I had ever seen; and if that's all there was, I was damn good and ready for the meaningless death part.

"I wasn't demanding, or threatening, or even pleading at that point. I just needed to know, and I needed to know *now*, or I couldn't go on anymore. When I came up here, when I got here, I thought I wanted to die here, and that was fine by me."

My eyes swam into focus, and they locked on his, and I whispered in the stillness of the cave:

"But I didn't. I came here to find the answer to my prayer. I came here to find you."

For the first time ever I saw Somebody get flustered. His face flushed and he looked away quickly with a stuttered little laugh.

"Well, no, not me *specifically*," he rushed to explain. "Don't transfer the importance of the message onto the messenger. I'm no saint, no angel. I'm not aiming to be crucified any time soon and I'm certainly not ready to quietly ascend once my time with you is through."

Eyes coming back to mine, he relaxed when he saw my smile.

"But you're wrong, and you know it," I said evenly, still smiling. "You *are* a saint, you *are* an angel, you *are* God, *you are everything*…" I gestured at the beautiful landscape, which seemed to glow all the more brightly, right on cue, "and *I* am everything, and *everything is God*. Goddess. The Universe. Whatever." I was mocking him, but I was beginning to understand him, too.

"And even if you jump on your Harley and ride off into this very sunset, never to be seen again, I'll still know that on the deepest level of my being. In fact, nothing can ever cause me not to know that again."

I felt that ever-more-familiar presence welling

up inside me as I spoke through the frog in my throat: "Ever."

Then I burst into tears.

* * *

Minutes later, on our backs in the still-wet grass, we munched on grass-stems and gazed contentedly skyward.

"I never told you I had a Harley," he mused aloud. "I've never even mentioned that I've ever ridden a motorcycle."

"Yeah, I know," I replied, just as calmly. "I didn't know it till I said it."

"But you knew it was true as surely as you knew what you said about the Infinite, and you were right. Did it feel magickal?"

I thought for a moment, reached out absently with my hand for a fresh grass-stem.

"*I* felt magickal," I replied, as I found the object of my quest with my blindly seeking hand and seized it gently. "The mind-reading or future-telling was but a happy by-product."

I expertly pulled the stem from its sleeve, placed it resolutely in my mouth and tossed its predecessor aside.

I was trying hard as I could to remain casual. It just didn't take.

"It *was* pretty cool, though, wasn't it?" I gushed, finally turning my head to look at him.

He laughed, glancing over at me.

"Yeah, it was pretty cool. And don't ever think it's not okay to be astounded and awed and excited. Around me or around anyone. If you can't be excited around the people that surround you, something's not right."

"And," I added wisely, "if you're not excited *by* the people that surround you and exciting *to* the people that surround you, there's something wrong as well."

He smiled at me, nodded. "You've learned that one already, have you?"

I shrugged, an awkward thing to do when you're halfway turned sideways, lying on your back.

"No, but I get the feeling that I will be soon."

He nodded, and we both went back to gazing at the sky.

Taken anew by the splendor of it all, I watched the occasional cloud drifting aimlessly across an otherwise clear and blue sky. As I felt a tear slip from the corner of my eye, he spoke softly:

"And what you said about never *not* knowing again, you meant that?"

"Absolutely," I whispered. Another tear followed the first.

"That will be tested, you know. By every person you meet, by every situation you encounter, and finally by the most miserable and heartbreaking period of your life you've ever experienced."

I looked at him, aghast, my peaceful reverie shattered. "I thought I just *went* through that."

He glanced at me a moment, looked off dreamily again.

"Sorry, kid. That was a cake walk compared to this."

I leaned up on one elbow, glared at him. "You're kidding me, right? I mean, I feel stronger and clearer and happier than I ever have in my life, than

I ever knew I could. I'm going to forget what I've learned? Is that what you're saying?"

He still wouldn't look at me. "Nobody, what I'm saying is that you will experience a time when nothing in your life seems to make sense, and you will experience the deepest torment you've ever experienced during this time. And the only thing you *will* have is what you know, what you've learned, what you've felt. You'll cling to it with all your might, you'll learn it inside and out, and it will be what enables you to survive."

Heaving a sigh, he tried to sound encouraging. "You feel strong and clear and happy now, and that's good. Enjoy it completely and remember it as clearly as possible. It will be what you need the most, that memory, when you go through what I'm talking about. This happens to virtually everyone who decides to delve more deeply into life and into themselves, and if by some rare miracle it doesn't happen to you I'll happily eat my words. But when it does, remember: it doesn't last forever, and it's infinitely better when you're done than it was when you started."

I resolved then and there to be the rare miracle, to have my hardest times behind me and to build solidly and continually on the precious new gems of knowledge I had discovered. My friend had never been wrong about anything, but he was going to be wrong about this.

Happy with my resolution, I promptly forgot that entire portion of the conversation. And having done so, I drifted peacefully off to sleep there under the sun on the still-wet grass.

CHAPTER TEN

"I've a game for us to play," he announced brightly as he bounced into the room one morning. "A game of intrigue and mystique, magick and intuition."

I looked up from my book, cocked an eyebrow at him. "Already I'm suspicious."

He feigned a hurt look, and I laughed. "How do we play?"

"I say something, you tell me whether or not it passes the test of intuition. If you feel yourself flinch inside, say 'no.' If you feel all warm and fuzzy inside, say 'yes.' Fun, huh?" Eagerness lit his face, and I couldn't help but smile and nod.

"Shoot," I said.

We sat facing each other, and he looked me in the eye.

"Life is hard in this world, and suffering inevitable."

I frowned. "No."

"People get old and feeble, and then they die. It's quite simply a fact of life."

"God, I hope not." He glared sternly at me. "Sorry. No."

"Love is not just a feeling but a power, a power that dissolves all negativity on contact."

"Yes! Hell yes!" This was fun.

"We draw into our lives every event, every person, every moment, every minuscule aspect of everything we see and hear and think and touch and smell and feel and taste and dream and—"

"Yes! Yes already!"

"Everybody's got to have a job; whether you like it or not, you've just got to put your nose to the grindstone and suffer through it or you'll starve. The sooner you accept that the better off you'll be."

I started crying. I didn't mean to, but next thing I knew sobs shook my shoulders and tears stained my face.

He looked at me, eyes wide.

"I used to believe that," I choked. "I used to believe all those terrible things, the job, the pain, the death."

Suddenly I was angry, the tears stopped. "Why did everybody tell me all those terrible things? Why do the people who are supposed to be there to help, to teach, lie about everything that's most important? Why, Goddammit?!"

The tears came again, and I buried my face in my hands.

I felt his hand fall gently on my shoulder. I looked up.

"Nobody," he said, his voice thick with emotion, "you mean your parents, your teachers, your friends?"

I nodded, not trusting my voice.

"And what do you think their parents and teachers and friends told them from day one?"

"Probably the same crap, the same hurtful lies, or at least their version of it," I snapped, angry again.

"And if you had had a child or children before learning what you came here to learn, what sort of environment would they have grown up in? What would they have learned from their loving father?"

I felt the tension, the anger, drain from my face.

"Oh, my God," I said, horrified.

He smiled. "They didn't lie to you, and they didn't teach you such things out of spite, or to hurt you. They gave you their highest truth, the best way they knew, the *only* way they knew to get along in the world. They were human beings, as far as they knew, and so were you. They just wanted you to learn the rules that inevitably apply to human beings."

"But I'm *not* a human being," I growled.

He shrugged. "Neither are they. Now you know it. Someday they will too, even if they wait until the day they die. And if they do see it sooner, if they approach you with an apology on their lips and tears in their eyes…?"

My own eyes filled with tears. "I'll tell them I understand now, that I'm not angry anymore." As I said it, I felt it. "I'll tell them the forgiveness I worked so hard to find was a sham, because there is no such thing as forgiveness, that understanding can be gained only through the attainment of a higher perspective. That understanding makes forgiveness look primitive."

He gawked at me.

"Right?"

He exploded from his seat, exasperated.

"Nobody! You speak so clearly with the voice of your own intuition and then ask for verification from me?! Ask yourself!"

I closed my eyes, thought of what I had just said.

"Yeah, you're right," I agreed. "I'm right."

Settling back into his seated position, he was the picture of calm. "That's better."

We sat a moment in silence, and I saw his eyes look past me, past the walls, past today. He looked so thoughtful, almost sad. Then his eyes snapped suddenly into focus once again, and he spoke slowly, evenly:

"That is what you'll need when you leave here, more than anything. Your intuition. People will want more than ever to knock you down a peg or two, to see in your eyes the misery that shows so plainly in theirs. You will want to share these things you're just beginning to see with everyone you meet. But most folks won't see you trying to help, they'll see you challenging the perspective they've spent their whole lives cultivating."

He sighed heavily. "And their knee-jerk response will be to in turn challenge your perspective. You will find yourself accused more and more often of living in a fantasy world the more clearly you learn to perceive reality. Your only source of truth, whether alone or surrounded by people claiming to act in your best interest, will be your intuition. If you feel, deep within, that what you are doing or saying or hearing or thinking is uplifting and wonderful and beautiful, follow it. If you feel uncomfortable, on any level; look within, and you will discover why. You are never alone, you are never lost, and you are never confused when you have learned to develop and pay close attention to your intuition every moment of every day."

I studied him carefully. "Am I going somewhere?" I loved it here, I loved this man, I loved the way I felt, the way we talked and the things we talked about…

"Everything is going somewhere, always," he replied. "If you will but look within, you will find that you are absolutely bursting with anticipation."

It was true, too. Life was different now, I was different now; and I wanted to see how it worked, living like this. But…

"But this is the first time I've met someone who doesn't make me want to run as fast and as far as I can from them." A frown creased my forehead, as I thought of leaving and thought of staying.

He laughed. "It won't be the last time," he predicted. "And I'm not kicking you out. You're not such bad company yourself."

I flushed, and he went on:

"But don't feel like you're insulting me wanting to leave. I'd be insulted if you didn't. I want to be the wind at your back, not the crutch by your side. Soon you will see that it's time to stop being 'Nobody' and start being the new and improved Jay Norry."

I started. He knew my name. Of course. I realized I had no reason to be surprised. He'd known it all along.

Not noticing my reaction, he was still talking. "You'll go the moment you're ready, just like you came the moment you were ready. Someday you'll even be making these decisions consciously, with full awareness on levels within yourself that you have yet to discover."

"Who *are* you?" I'd asked before, but I had to ask again.

He didn't answer right away. After a moment's thought, he smiled finally.

"I'm nobody," he replied, "pretending to be somebody for a while for the sake of a dear friend on his way to becoming somebody himself." He laughed at his own riddle. "To settle a debt of sorts."

I was more confused than ever. Puzzled, I asked him how he could owe me when we had never even met before.

"Time, my friend, is not what you believe it to be. You'll know that soon enough, and you might even set some lost and confused soul on the road to knowing it too. And maybe he'll prove it to you."

He would say nothing more on the subject, no matter how I pressed him.

"I don't understand," I said finally, "But somehow I do." He inclined his head slightly. "Thank you, my friend."

Reaching out, he patted my hand. "Thank *you*." He stood up. "And goodnight."

Yawning hugely, I realized suddenly how tired I was.

"G'night," I said casually. I had the sudden urge to say more; to think of something, anything, to keep him talking all night if I could. I couldn't explain it though, and I shrugged it off.

Sleep came quickly, easily, and I gave it no more thought.

CHAPTER ELEVEN

I awoke the next morning with a start. *Something was wrong.*

Sitting up quickly, instantly alert, I hit my head just as I opened my eyes.

I was in my car. And I had a knot on my head from where I had hit my head on the glass earlier. Months earlier…

The lump wasn't more than a few hours old. I laughed out loud suddenly. Then I started crying, happy tears rolling down my cheeks as it all fell together.

I had prayed.

Then I had gone somewhere, just where I needed to go. Another plane, an alternate Earth, a convenient little skip in time…

I'd call it a dream, though, if anyone ever pressed for an explanation…not just because I didn't fully understand, but because somehow I did, and that's all that mattered.

Yes, a dream…

A dream that lasted some five months, five months that stood out more clearly and more vividly than any other time in my life…

A dream that opened my eyes in so many ways, that had changed me "overnight" into a completely different person…

A dream that had introduced me to the best friend I'd ever had…

Yeah, I'd call it a dream, if anybody asked.

Decision made, I wiped the tears from my eyes; but I couldn't wipe the smile from my face. I got out of my car, saw the same group of people who'd heard me swearing in despair some other time and some other place so much like this one.

It was a family, parents just taking their children to the store. The parents turned their heads at the sound of my car door opening.

"Howdy!" I hollered, waving at them wildly like they were my best friends in the world. And they *were*. They were my brothers and sisters, and they glowed so brightly, and I loved them so.

The adults crowded their children closer to them, the man giving me a curt nod and uttering a greeting I couldn't hear, then quickly herding his family toward the store.

I almost burst out laughing, but I knew they'd take that wrong as well. A part of me wanted to run after them, yelling, "No, no, it's okay! I love you, I love *everything*! Don't you see?!"

But I was all too familiar with the world I'd grown up in. Running after perfect strangers with proclamations of love on your lips just plain old isn't cool, no matter how well you may have slept.

I realized then that I must still look like that

walking-dead drugged-out wastoid I'd seen staring back at me from the river that day. I reached into my car before closing the door and grabbed my baseball cap. I pulled the bill down low, almost over my eyes.

I pressed the goofy smile I felt on my mouth down as much as possible, ended up with a just-as-goofy lopsided grin.

I laughed, shrugged, then walked to the store.

It was pandemonium inside. A wall of too-loud sound and too-bright lights slammed into me, and I stood there dazed for a moment too long.

I could hear their thoughts. I could *feel* what they were feeling. I could see an ethereal glow surrounding everyone.

And I knew better than to start grabbing people at random by the shoulders, shaking them, crying out, "You are so *beautiful*, don't you see?!"

Yes, I knew better. And that's the only reason I didn't do it.

Instead, I feigned adjusting my cap so I could wipe away the tear that had appeared mysteriously and happily under my right eye.

I was desperately hungry, and I wandered among the neatly stacked food a good two minutes before I remembered that I hadn't a dime to my name.

"No, not quite right," I muttered under my breath as I walked by the chips and dips and soda pop on my way to the exit. "There's seventy-eight cents on the floor of my car, I'll betcha."

As the automatic door opened in front of me, I had a moment to wonder at how happy I felt, how totally unafraid I felt. I'd never in my life been so completely broke, so completely alone, or so seemingly without options. Yet I knew with the whole of my being that everything was going to be all right. That it already was.

As I walked through the open doorway, I spoke aloud again, under my breath: "I mean, c'mon, it's just not like the Universe to let its newly reborn child starve."

There was a middle-aged, stocky man kneeling down momentarily to retrieve something from the vending machine just outside the door.

He glanced up at the sound of my voice. "What was that?"

"Nothing," I smiled. "Sorry, just talking to myself."

He smiled, looked down at the candy bar in his hand, looked up at me, then tossed it underhand to me.

I caught it deftly, looked down at it. Snickers, my favorite. I looked back at him.

He shrugged. "Thought I wanted it." He turned and walked away, then called back over his shoulder: "Thought wrong. G'day."

I looked up at the beautiful sunless overcast sky, said a quick holy-shit-that-was-awfully-cool-of-you-thanks-a-bunch-prayer in my mind, felt it in my heart...

Then I ate the candy bar in three bites.

There was a bank of pay phones not three steps away.

My parents weren't very happy to hear from me, and I didn't blame them. They didn't know the specifics of my life since I moved out, but even a vague picture wasn't a pretty one.

It took two phone calls; they were divorced now. They were both reluctant, and understandably so; but my Dad said to call back later.

I didn't worry, oddly enough, not for a moment. I kept marveling at that. All my friends were either strung out on crank or living in caves in alternate dimensions…

But I wouldn't have been surprised if a complete stranger had walked up and handed me a hundred-dollar bill.

Grateful, yes. Surprised? No.

The next phone call yielded the inevitable news, though; and I was armed with pen and paper to take down the address he was going to wire the money to. First he had some conditions, though, as I had expected:

"I'm only sending you this money if you're going to use it to come home," he started.

"I know," I replied, "and I am. And before you say anything, I want to tell you that you don't have to worry about the drugs. I'm done with them, and they're done with me. And I'll pay you back, I've always had a good job…" I paused. "Until now. I just need a little help getting back on my feet again."

"Okay. Good. Then come home."

He gave me the address, then asked if I had enough gas to get there. It was a Renton address, not far at all.

"Yeah, I've got seventy-eight cents in my car,"

I giggled, then bit my wrist to keep from laughing. "What?"

"Nothing. Thanks, Dad. I appreciate it, I really do." I did, too. We said our goodbyes, and I went back to my car.

Minutes later, I laid my seventy-eight cents quietly on the counter in front of the same girl who hadn't said a word to me on this very same day so long ago.

I looked her in the eye, smiled softly. "Beautiful day, isn't it?" I mused.

"It's *raining*," she scowled. "Whaddya want?"

"Seventy-eight cents on pump number four and a smile would just make my day." I winked at her.

She smiled wanly. "Sorry. Rain burns me out. Pump four, you said?"

I nodded. "And I would be utterly delighted if you would promise to smile like that at least three more times today. I bet you make at least one more person's day. It really is a beautiful smile."

She beamed at me. "Thank *you*, sir! You have a wonderful day." I gave her a thumbs-up on my way out.

The gas was pumping, and I was checking the pressure in my tires when she came rushing out of the store. I knew what was wrong right away, and I shut the pump off before the door had even closed behind her.

The digital read-out stood at just under three dollars. We looked at each other over the roof of my car.

"Fine," she said playfully. "I'll promise to smile today if you'll promise to come back and offer to pay the two dollars and nineteen cents you owe this gas station within the next…five years."

I placed my hand over my heart in a spontaneous gesture of sincerity. "I promise."

She smirked, whirled around and headed back into the store.

"Thank you!" I called laughingly to her as she disappeared through the doorway.

I had some errands to run; I had today to live all over again, any way I pleased.

* * *

It was early evening before I was back in my car, with a tankful of gas, headed east on I-90.

I was twenty-one years old, I had my whole long life ahead of me…and I had so many reasons to live. Finally. It didn't feel like a second chance, it felt like a first chance.

Before I even crested Snoqualmie Pass, I knew I had to stop for a good, hot, healthy dinner. I was more than halfway through, trying to savor every bite (but more or less gobbling it down eagerly), when I heard a strange sound.

For this time of year, anyway.

It was a Harley-Davidson; anyone who even *likes* Harleys knows the sound of one immediately. It was *January*, we were at the *summit* of the pass; and some guy was pulling up on a *motorcycle*.

I raised my water glass in a silent toast to the guy's determination just as he killed the engine outside. A moment later he stood in the doorway, shaking off the cold, his leathers creaking.

It was him… He was real… It hadn't been a dream!

I was on my feet without thinking, napkin falling unnoticed from my lap. I dashed up to him and crushed him in a monstrous bear hug, nearly lifting him off his feet.

His frame was stiff and awkward in my embrace. I let go of him, stepped back. Then I saw his eyes.

They were sad; miserable, even. Torment shone in them in such depth that tears welled up in my own eyes.

And he didn't recognize me.

In the same instant I saw these things, I also saw that there was no gray in his hair or beard; the lines around his eyes were faint, and had yet to turn into laugh lines. They were more like lines caused by constantly squinting, trying to look close enough to see what you knew was there but had yet to glimpse for the first time.

Like he was squinting at me right now.

Thankful for my quick new mind, I was able to assimilate all this in a split second.

I took another step back, inclined my head respectfully, and said, "My apologies, friend. I had just been thinking of a very dear friend whom you happen to bear a remarkable resemblance to. When you walked through the door, it surprised me so much I lost my composure a bit. I apologize."

He held up his hand, gave me a weak smile. "No apology necessary. No harm done."

He may have been a little older and a boatload wiser when I'd known him before, but I still liked him instantly.

"Well," I said quickly, before he had a chance to walk away, "since you know I'm not a nutjob, and since we both seem to be flying solo this evening…" I gestured to my booth, "…may I buy you a hot meal and perhaps make a friend?"

I didn't have much money, no; but I had enough set aside for a motel room. And if this guy had a hankering for steak and lobster, I'd gladly sleep in my car tonight.

He looked at me strangely, and I was reminded suddenly of when he had asked me to stay just a week, to prove what he had to prove.

Then he smiled. "Actually, I just stopped in for a cup of coffee. But you can certainly buy me that."

We sat down, and he gestured for me to finish my meal. "In a minute," I said. "I want you to talk to me while I eat."

He glanced at me over the rim of his coffee cup. "About what?"

I shrugged. "Oh, you know…" I let my eyes wander the ceiling, "What you've learned, what makes you tick, why you're here…"

Coffee placed gently on the table, he looked at me square. "You don't want to hear that kind of shit from someone like me, kid," he said firmly. "What I've learned isn't pretty."

"But I do. Please." I tried to convey my sincerity as best I could.

He thought for a moment. "How much time you got?"

"All the time in the world." I spread my hands. "You?"

"Me too."

Then he started talking, and I started eating, and he told me what he had seen.

I wondered for a moment if the joke was on him, asking him to talk while I ate; or if the joke had been on me, when he had asked me not to. I shrugged it off, and knew that I didn't taste another bite either way.

His words painted a picture of a hard life. We had never spoken of his life during our time together; I had always assumed that he couldn't understand what kind of pain I was talking about, that that was why he always brushed it away when I tried to wallow in it. He had never mentioned how much he had endured, and I'd never been able to picture him as anything but clear and happy.

A childhood alternating between abuse and neglect, filled with nothing but pain and guilt, it made mine look healthy in comparison. He hadn't brushed away my pain because he couldn't understand it; he had brushed it away because I had so little to work through. I listened to him intently as he spoke of it, dispassionate and earnest at the same time, recounting events and his own feelings.

He went on, reluctant at first, but getting steadily more comfortable as the pain and guilt of his younger years gave way to an adolescence that made one yearn for the simple pain and guilt of childhood. I kept waiting for him to get to the part where he was institutionalized – when it finally broke him.

But he didn't. I watched his memories through his words, as he pushed himself harder and harder to overcome it, to succeed as an adult as completely as he had watched others fail. But it fell apart every time it seemed to be coming together, on a frustratingly precise timetable of about once every seven years.

"I thought I'd finally done it," he said as the waitress cleared my dishes and refilled our coffee cups. "I had it all: my own business, a beautiful wife, a nice house, my dream ride." He stole a glance at his Harley outside, as I had seen him do a half-dozen times during his monologue.

"But I'd forgotten the seven year cycle," he said

bitterly. "Every time I build my life up better than before; and every seven years I lose it all, no matter what I do."

He looked again at his Harley.

"I love that bike," he said softly. "Sometimes I ride around for hours, pretend I'm headed somewhere incredibly important, to do something that will truly make a difference."

I smiled. "Significantly changing lives for the better everywhere you parked for a time."

His eyes widened, and he nodded. "Yeah. Y'know, I've never told anybody this, and you might think I'm a little crazy, but…when I'm on my bike, time seems to stretch and spin and fold back on itself. It feels sometimes like I'll pull up in my driveway someday just to see myself pulling out. I feel more surprised when it doesn't happen than I would feel if it did.

"I like to think that I could use that, that I could ride back or forward in time, to anywhere and any*when* I choose…ride into some friend or loved one's life at just the right time, to tell them just what they need to hear at just the crucial moment when they need to hear it. Whether it's 'don't step out in front of that car next Tuesday or you'll never walk again,' or just a few choice words of encouragement."

He looked away, a little embarrassed. "Sorry, I know it's nuts. I just—"

"Don't sell your bike," I said suddenly.

"What?"

I was excited suddenly, bursting with it, talking fast. "Look, your marriage is over, your business self-destructed, and you'll never keep the house. Right?"

He frowned. "I was getting to that, yeah."

"Whatever you do, don't sell your bike," I insisted. "It's not a luxury, it's your little piece of magick. Everyone needs that in their lives, at least just a little bit."

"This was going to be our last ride," he said. "That's why I'm riding in the middle of winter; I was going to sell her next week, to buy myself a little reprieve."

He placed his hands resolutely on the table, on either side of his coffee cup. "You're right, kid. I'll keep my baby, no matter what. No trade-down, no compromise. I'll keep her."

I beamed at him.

"Any other suggestions?" He smiled wryly.

"How much time you got?"

He laughed for the first time, a real laugh; and I had to fight the urge to jump up and hug him again, he reminded me so much of the man who had saved my life.

"All the time in the world, kid. All the time in the world."

For the next two hours we talked intently, an abridged version of the months I had just spent with him.

Only this time he had all the questions, and I had all the answers.

He was so excited, so open, and so much quicker to catch on than I had been.

After the waitress had come to tell us they'd be closing soon, he seized my hand across the table, grasped it firmly.

"How do you know all this stuff?" he asked me suddenly.

Tears welled up in my eyes, and I smiled slowly. "Somebody took the time to teach me."

"Next time you see him, be sure to thank him for me," he whispered.

Squeezing his hand, I smiled. "Be happy, be clear, and have fun, my friend."

I got up to pay the check, and as I waited for the cashier I turned to him.

"Remember what you said about time seeming to stretch and spin and fold back on itself when you're riding?" I asked. He nodded. "I think you may be onto something there."

The cashier came then, and I turned away again before I saw his reaction.

I walked back to the table, shook his hand again. "We'll meet again, my friend; I'm sure of it. In the meantime I get the feeling you'll learn a great deal more than I know now."

I turned to walk away, but he called after me as my hand fell on the door handle.

I stopped, turned to face him.

"Who are you?" he asked.

"Who, me?" I grinned. "I'm Nobody. Nice ta meetcha."

I gave him a solemn salute and then stepped out into the bitter cold. I skipped playfully to my car, got in and cranked the heat. Then I pointed my car east on I-90 once again, to begin the first of my many adventures in being human.

For, you see, I was no longer a human being.

EPILOGUE

I burst through the front door out into the chill Montana air as if someone were chasing me with a knife. But no one was chasing me, and the threat was not to my life…it was a threat to my clarity.

Breathing deeply, watching the fog escaping my lips, I clutched my head violently between my hands. These people were impossible! I had watched every conversation I had had with everyone I had tried to have it with fall flat on its face before my very eyes.

After so many months of such easy depth and clarity with Somebody, I had come to feel that that was natural. But people didn't want to discuss this; they seemed to…they seemed to want to avoid it at all cost.

No, no, I couldn't believe that. It must be my approach, it must be the way I said what I said. I had to learn to be patient, to make my point more clearly.

Spreading my arms, I leaned my head back, looked to the sky.

"What?!" I shouted. "What am I supposed to do, what am I supposed to say?!"

I couldn't just keep it all hidden; even when I was quiet I made people uncomfortable. "What are you smiling about? What are you so happy about?"

Such questions, and thrown at me like accusations. And to answer them honestly was even worse; "Well, good for you, Mister Perfect. I don't see you walking on water," or "You're not better than me, you know. 'All men are created equal.'"

My happiness made me feel like the loneliest man on Earth. Not that I wanted to trade it, mind you…I just didn't imagine it would be so hard to share.

"What?!" I yelled again at the unanswering sky.

Then, like a ton of bricks, it fell upon me from within. I laughed, I cried, I breathed it in and I loved it. None of it mattered, nothing mattered but this. I literally jumped for joy, arms still outstretched. I was weightless, I was LOVE, I was…

I was floating.

I felt it, all through me, and somehow it didn't surprise me at all to look down and see the snow two feet under my feet. The feeling was the incredible part, the FEELING made all things possible; it was natural, it was right…wait a minute!

The moment the thought hit my mind, my feet hit the ground. My knees buckled and I let myself fall face-first into the snow. I lay there laughing for a moment.

Then I collected myself, caught myself looking around almost guiltily to see if anyone had witnessed it. There was no one in sight. I sighed, as relieved as I was disappointed.

On my knees in the snow, I let myself feel the gratitude welling up, the happiness that caused it and seemed to be caused *by* it.

Then, smiling softly, I stood and walked back to the house. Everything was going to be fine.

In fact, it already was.

IF YOU ONLY KNEW

If only you knew who you really are, you would laugh more.

If only you knew where we really are from, you would cry more too...not hopeless tears of fear, but shameless tears of love.

If only you knew how utterly unimportant everything is, you would see just how important everything truly can be.

If only you knew that you're not what you do, not what you say, not what you feel...you'd do so much more, see it so clear, feel it so pure.

If only you knew what I'm trying to say, we'd dance with pure joy, laughing for hours at our own unrealistic happiness.

If only you knew what I can't make words say...

If only you knew...each moment, each day...

If only you knew that none of it's true...

If only you knew, if only you knew...

Jay Norry – June 10, 1997

Also available from J.K. Norry. . .

Dreaming The Perpetual Dream

The Ringer
Ringing in a Voyage
Ringing in a New Year

Zombie Zero
Zombie Zero: The First Zombie
Zombie Zero: The Last Zombie

Zombie Zero: The Short Stories
Volume 1: The Sickness Spreads
Volume 2: The Beginning of the End
Volume 3: Love Lost at Sea
Volume 4: The Zombie Killers
Volume 5: Monstrous Consequences
Volume 6: The Heart of the Monster

Walking Between Worlds
Demons & Angels (Book I)
Rise of the Walker King (Book II)
Fall of the Walker King (Book III)
The Demon Be Damned

As Jay Norry
Words Are Made Up!
Earth Is In Space!
Stumbling Backasswards Into the Light

Learn more about the author at **www.JayNorry.com**

www.ingramcontent.com/pod-product-compliance
Lightning Source LLC
Chambersburg PA
CBHW031425290426
44110CB00011B/530